Inner
by Lin

Lin, with her husband, Ralph.

Inner Vision

by

Lin Berwick

with a Foreword by Denis Duncan

Arthur James

BOOK PUBLISHERS

Acknowledgement is made to The Drummond Trust, 3 Pitt Terrace, Stirling, Scotland, for their supporting the publication of this book.

First published in 1990
by Arthur James Limited
One Cranbourne Road, London, N10 2BT, England

British Library Cataloguing in Publication Data
Berwick, Lin, *1950-*
    Inner vision.
    1. England. Blind spastic persons: Berwick, Lin, 1950-
    I. Title
    362.41092

ISBN 0-85305-306-5

Cover by The Creative House, Saffron Walden, Essex

Typeset in Frankfurt by Christel Ivo
Printed by The Guernsey Press Co. Ltd.,
Guernsey, Channel Islands

CONTENTS

DEDICATION

To my darling husband Ralph,

with love

ACKNOWLEDGMENTS

I should like sincerely to thank the Rev. Dr. Denis Duncan, Managing Director of Arthur James Limited, who commissioned this book, because writing it made me take a fresh look at my life and helped me to see just how much God has been with me throughout the years. I have, in writing this book, seen how all things work together for good, even though it may not always seem like it at the time. I have come to realise that everything is part of God's rich pattern.

I owe a great debt of gratitude to Christina Wilson who has given me a tremendous amount of help with the typing and editing of the text. She has been a wonderful advisor and general sounding-board. Her comments on what I had written were something I greatly valued. Working on this text has brought us closer to one another and this, for me, has been a very precious gift from God.

I thank too the three well-known broadcasters who have written tributes for this book — Sue MacGregor of the BBC Radio Today programme, Rosemary Anne Sisson, the author of *Upstairs, Downstairs,* and Joan Shenton of Capital Radio. I also thank Dr Wendy Greengross for her kind words.

I should also want to thank my husband Ralph for the way in which he has supported me during the writing of this book. He has helped in so many ways — reading and correcting the text, holding back many an evening meal so that I could work with Christina, coping with my mood changes when it was difficult for me to write down painful memories. The time we spent with this project has been very special. Without his love and support it would have been extremely difficult to complete it.

The events in this book are not necessarily in chronological order, as my purpose is to illustrate how God has used my life to its fullest extent, to fulfil his 'rich pattern'.

All through my life I have been aware of the power of God guiding and controlling me, displaying all too clearly how He wants to use the dark as well as the joyful periods. Adversity can be changed to joy so long as we accept the will of God.

TRIBUTES

Lin Berwick is one of the most remarkable people I know. We first met a dozen or so years ago, when I was the presenter of *Woman's Hour* on BBC radio and Lin rang me — one of her most endearing characteristics is that she is not at all backward in persuading people to join her in getting things done — to ask if we might talk together for Moorfields Radio, the eye hospital's radio service in London. I agreed to do this if Lin would come to Broadcasting House to record our interview; little did I know before we met, and Lin certainly didn't tell me over the phone, how physically handicapped she is. But one of the marvellous things about her is that, from the moment she is with you — she is wheelchair-bound for much of the time because of her cerebral palsy, *and* blind — you are hardly aware of her disabilities. At the time she was working as a telephonist at a bank in the City of London.

Not long after that she wrote her first book, *Undefeated,* and came in to talk about it on *Woman's Hour.* Lin tells me that one of her chief memories of the occasion was eating Christmas cake — our recipe of the week! My recollections of her then are of an extraordinarily cheerful, articulate and resourceful woman who is not at all sorry for herself; I know these qualities apply even more now. She has also gained a marvellous husband, several stepchildren and step-grandchildren, and some brand-new pursuits, not the least of which is running the Lin Berwick Trust. This book tells the story so far.

Sue MacGregor

I first met Lin Berwick on the telephone when she rang to suggest interviewing me on the Moorfield Hospital radio. She mentioned that she was blind as we made arrangements to meet. She remarked that she didn't walk very well, either.

"That's not fair!" I said.

"No, that's what I thought!" she replied, and we both laughed heartily.

We have been friends ever since.

Soon after I met Lin, my mother had a bad fall, and for the first time I became aware of the sickening crassness and selfishness of the fit and well. Cars were parked across slopes intended for wheel-chairs; doors were too heavy; stairs barred every access. (Just try going to the National Theatre in a wheel-chair!) But, while I was jumping up and down, yelling with rage, my mother smiled and was courteous, remaining staunchly herself. Like Lin.

Since that first telephone meeting, Lin has become something of a celebrity, an author, a counsellor, and a Methodist Lay Preacher. She has acquired further independence through marriage. I know too well how tough the day-to-day physical and spiritual stresses of life must be for her, but what matters most to us, as to her, is that she remains her own delightful, tough, funny self. She has written this book, and I can't wait to read it.

Rosemary Anne Sisson

I first spoke to Lin Berwick on the telephone in 1973. Those were the heady days of Capital Radio when Tommy Vance and I were doing an early show called *Swap Shop*.

We had raised some money from our generous listeners through a snowball auction on air and were looking for someone to benefit. An article in the East London Advertiser described how Lin Berwick, founder of the Disabled Fellowship Club of East London, needed money for a second ambulance for her group.

This articulate, self-confident young woman at the other end of the telephone made all the arrangements with great efficiency. It was only later when we met that I realised the extent of Lin's physical disability. She is totally blind and cerebral palsied, able to walk only a few steps with two tripod sticks.

I use the word disability reluctantly for want of another, but in fact Lin has never been disabled. She has done everything she set her mind on doing with the help of her loving parents and by manipulating everybody within earshot!

She persuaded me to become Vice President of the Disabled Fellowship Club and we became firm friends. Together we had many adventures. We took part in radio programmes, I as a guest on her show on Moorfields Hospital Radio, and she as a guest on *Person to Person* at Capital Radio. We opened a Jobcentre in Chiswick together and I had the fun of helping the *This Is Your Life* team surprise her when she was the deserving subject of that programme.

Lin has taught me many lessons. She is immensely talented. Amongst her many gifts is the 'gift of the gab'.

She is a naturally talented public speaker and broadcaster with the ability to speak eloquently 'off the cuff' and carries great authority when speaking, as she so often does, on behalf of the community of other disabled people who are so close to her heart.

Joan Shenton

I first met Lin in 1975 when she was going through a very difficult time as she was having severe pain in her remaining eye and facing up to the terrible finality of realising that her eye would have to be removed.

Since that time I have seen her develop, coping with her own personal problems and difficulties with immense courage and cheerfulness and being not only able to make her own necessary adjustments but also increasingly offering help and spiritual strength to others who need help. In her association with *Carematch*, she gave not only a total commitment and enthusiasm, but also unstinting loyalty in devoting out-of-work hours to publicity talks and fund raising.

Lin is a most unusual person and it has been a pleasure and a privilege to know her. She is travelling a remarkable journey.

Wendy Greengross

FOREWORD

L I N
by Denis Duncan

One of the great but humbling privileges of my ministry has been the opportunity to meet with outstanding people in every walk of life. Were I to compile a list of their names, it would include the great and the good, the famous and the unknown, the scholar, the academic, the entertainer, the saint, and perhaps too the not so saintly. I mentioned this background of acquaintance only to try to place Lin Berwick in context. I have to conclude, and gladly do, that for courage and conviction she is, in my experience, unsurpassed. My admiration for Lin, my respect for her ability and my joy in her manifold successes know no bounds. She is amazing.

My contact with Lin spans a decade. It also involves a variety of associations. I met her first when she came to Westminster Pastoral Foundation to train in counselling of a psychotherapeutic kind. In my role there as Associate Director and Training Supervisor, I had her in my care and saw at first hand the extraordinary way in which she tackled that enormous task. She writes about it in this book. To that I shall return.

When I had the responsibility as Director of The Churches' Council for Health and Healing of making a video on 'The Healing Ministry', it was to Lin that I turned to help us illustrate the great theme of healing through suffering. Thousands of people have seen that video and have been deeply moved by the fifteen minutes or so when Lin spoke of her journey, not to the physical cure which lay outside the realm of possibility and miracle, but her journey towards wholeness through cerebral palsy and blindness, that is through pain and suffering. She continues to witness, in her preaching ministry, to the journey towards wholeness that we are all called to make.

Having now had to undertake the management and direction of this publishing house, Arthur James Limited, I find myself extending Lin's ministry in yet another way. I do this with pleasure and satisfaction. I am glad to provide a way for many other people, and especially those who need encouragement, to encounter Lin Berwick.

The last thing I dare do is introduce any 'slushy senti-mentality' (Lin's phrase) into this foreword. This she would not tolerate, as I know so well. I stay then with hard fact and objective assessment.

Lin's story is an incredible one. How can a multipli-disabled young woman possibly overcome difficulties as she has done? Take on 'authority', sadly so often negative in its attitude towards her, and win? Keep her vision clear despite barriers, obstacles and discouragements? It all comes from the 'inner vision' that is a product of her personal faith. Her spiritual eyes are bright and shining! She sees clearly what God would have her do. She has followed her star and found the Lord.

I am especially glad that, in her husband Ralph, she has recently found the exceptional, loving support that enables her to "fight the good fight" (one of her favourite hymns) and "run the straight race". Her marriage has done so much to bring her fulfilment as a woman.

The story Lin tells of her rejection at Westminster Pastoral Foundation involves me. It is an important story for, in the decision of the Training Committee which I had to take to Lin, she experienced her most bitter blow. I conveyed that crucial decision — one of the hardest things I have ever had to do — being the executive of the body which had to make such decisions and stand by them. I felt the decision to be wrong, as I made clear at the time, but it was the corporate majority decision of the Committee by which we were all bound. There is no need for me to try and explain or justify that decision. What is important is that Lin should feel free to tell her story and express her feelings about the episode, and that she does in this book. As I have said, the rejection brought her greatest crisis, certainly the greatest disappointment and setback in her life. This is the story of how she has coped with such crises and triumphed over any obstacle placed in her way, always emerging victorious.

Undefeated is the title of her earlier book, now out of print. *Inner Vision* replaces that book and takes her story on to where she is today. That includes being a counsellor widely recognised for her abilities, used in that role both in a television programme and by a national newspaper in the disability field. Her present life proclaims her achievements. Her future life will demonstrate that there is more to emerge from such splendid 'inner vision'.

Having shared unwillingly the worst moment of her life, I have very willingly undertaken to bring Lin's story and witness to a yet wider public. She is known to many 'personalities' in the entertainment field. She became known to the nation through her appearance on *This Is Your Life*. She is known to so many people in pain through her counselling ministry. She has blessed many through her preaching ministry. To have the opportunity to support Lin in any way is a great privilege. The episode of pain we shared a decade ago, far from putting a barrier between us, has led onwards to mutual respect and affection. This further shared ministry in print is pure pleasure and real joy.

I hope that, moved by what you read in this book, you will feel you want to support Lin in *The Lin Berwick Trust,* just founded. You will read more of it as you come to the end of her story — her story so far, for Lin has much to do yet. The Trust is a concrete expression of the inner vision which drives Lin on. To support that Trust would be to express admiration for an extraordinary Christian.

Denis Duncan   May 10, 1990

Chapter One

Heeding the Call

I remember this, the most significant event in my life, as though it were yesterday. It was one Sunday in March, 1981. I attended the evening act of worship at Poplar Methodist Mission in the East End of London, just a few yards away from my home, as I usually did.

The service was in no sense remarkable but, when worship is conducted by the Rev. Bryan Rippin, you could guarantee that he would preach as though he had a Bible in one hand and the *Guardian* newspaper in the other! He preached with a social conscience and lived his Christianity in practical, everyday terms and he expected us to do the same. He championed causes relating to people from the East End of London, especially since its face had altered dramatically with the advent of Yuppyland and the Docklands Development. He proclaimed basic truths around the issues of the day. I could imagine that if Christ were preaching today, his stance would be much the same.

Over the two preceding years, I had been greatly influenced by Bryan Rippin. He had sown many seeds of faith in me and, almost imperceptibly, they had germinated within me. After the evening service people were standing around chatting and there was much activity. I was still seated in the pew, deep in my own thoughts, when I felt a hand on my left shoulder. I turned and asked "Who is there? Who wants to talk to me?" I heard a voice, deep in tone yet surrounded by an echo, which said "You have got to get off that seat and go to the front of the church and witness for me". I could not believe what I was hearing! I do not usually have a high sense of drama in my life, and I have certainly never before heard voices in my head! I felt a wonderful sense of peace and stillness, almost as if I had shut out all the extraneous noises around me. I was absolutely elated by the experience and was in no doubt at all that it was God speaking, loud and clear.

I went home that evening excited, happy and yet thoroughly confused by what had happened to me. I was in no doubt that I would ignore this call at my peril. I could not help wondering what I should do with such a command. The thought of preaching, and the study that it would involve, seemed for me — a multipli-disabled person — utterly daunting. What about all the practical issues — reading, finding the appropriate study material, compiling essays, the sheer physical problems of the accessibility of some of our churches, few of which were designed for disabled people? Often access is difficult enough for the worshipper, but it can be even more so for the preacher because of ascending to the pulpit (which would for me be a physical impossibility), the vestry where the access can be difficult and, in some churches, the problem of a fixed communion rail. The more I thought about it, the more I knew that, despite all these barriers, I could not ignore the call. I decided not to share what had happened with anyone for three weeks, until I had worked through some of these difficulties. I wrestled with the question "Why *me*? Why should God choose someone who is totally blind and suffers from cerebral palsy, walks with sticks and has to use a wheelchair over long distances?" I thought I would only be a nuisance and a burden to people and that my aspiration to preach would be regarded as totally ridiculous and absolutely impossible. But, right from the time when I was a small child, I knew that, despite everything, I had been given many blessings, not least of all the gifts of perfect speech and good clear intelligence, rare for someone with cerebral palsy. So why *not* me?

If we look at various passages in scripture we see that Jesus makes some of his strongest points through those who would have been regarded as the weaker members in the society of his day — the healing of the blind man, the man who was sick of the palsy, the man with the withered hand and the healing of Legion for example. All these people would have been seen as social outcasts, the non-achievers, and yet Jesus shows us what can be achieved by faith. If God gave me such a clear message, then it suggested that, if He wanted me to witness through my weakness, the obstacles confronting me would be overcome.

After my three weeks' meditation I went to Bryan Rippin and told him what had happened to me. He said, "But Lin, aren't you already witnessing through the work that you do with the disabled and your counselling of the bereaved? I suggest that you go away and think about it for another month. Then, if the conviction that you must preach remains with you, we will see what we can do about it." I did as he asked, but that conviction gained momentum. *I knew I had no choice.* I had to complete the task that God had set before me. I still wondered "Why *me*?" I hope I always shall, for when I lose that sense of wonder, that will be time to stop preaching. I hope I never lose my sense of incredulity and fear over my call, because I have always felt so strongly, now as then, the awesome responsibility I have to my congregation. We do not know how the things we say or do affect people and, in all that we do when communicating God's love, we should be aware of that fact.

One month later I went to Bryan and told him I was even more certain that I must preach and that nothing he could say or do would alter that fact. So it was decided that he would approach the Local Preachers' meeting to ask that I be given a "note to preach". That done, I started what was to be a seven-year programme with many false starts and pitfalls on the way before I achieved my goal of becoming a fully Accredited Methodist Local Preacher.

I should not have been surprised by my destiny because I had been given several signs along the road of my life which I want to share with you.

Chapter Two

My Friend, Jesus

To be asked to preach at the Poplar Methodist Mission only confirmed my conviction that I had a call to ministry. It was the church at which I had worshipped for most of my childhood. (It was then a Congregational Church). Christ has been my foundation and my support through-out my life. This was confirmation that I was being called to serve him as a minister.

When I was born, I was three months premature and spent the first twelve weeks of my life in an oxygen tent. With such a frail beginning — I weighed just 2lbs at birth — I knew that I had to fight to survive. In fact, during the first few minutes of my life the doctors regarded me as stillborn and directed their energies to attending to my mother. Suddenly I gave the tiniest squeak and then it was panic stations — and prayers — in an effort to keep me alive!

I know that this was a traumatic period for my parents. They had the daughter they dearly wanted, but their joy was tempered with extreme anxiety over my condition. Because I was close to death, it was decided that I should be baptised immediately by the hospital chaplain, so two West Indian nurses (whom, sadly, I have never met) acted as my godparents. Through that simple act of worship, my parents gave me a sense of belonging and a firm foundation in the Christian faith. The power of prayer was to play a most vital part in the weeks and years to come.

Eighteen months after my birth I was taken to see a neurologist who said bluntly: "This child is spastic. Take her home, forget about her, she will never be any good. You are wasting my time, your time and everybody else's". That statement devastated my family. It is difficult to break bad news but surely that news could have been conveyed with a little more sensitivity.

Today we do not refer to people as "being spastic". Rather we say that they are "brain-damaged" or that they suffer from cerebral palsy. I prefer to talk about cerebral palsy. The term "brain-damaged" is far more destructive because it conjures up images of the child being little more than a vegetable. Moreover, when specialists use a blanket-term like "brain-damaged" they should clarify it by providing as much detail as possible and especially the degree of damage that is known. When such news has to be conveyed, it is necessary to provide the parents or carer(s) with a positive approach to the child's disability so that this can be emphasised throughout the child's life. All too often we see disability in a totally negative light. We see the problems rather then the potential. In such circumstances we need to discover the abilities, the talents and the gifts of that disabled person.

The negative attitude of some able-bodied people, particularly among professionals, can be far more crippling than the disability itself. Christ did not label people in this way. He met them as they were and dealt with them at the stage of life which they had reached. The same attitude should be ours.

I have suffered throughout my life because of the attitudes of others. I have often been the object of a slushy sentimentality and much over-protectiveness. People have tended to wrap me up in cotton wool because they feel I have been hurt enough by what life has done to me. I want however to be allowed to take risks, to feel emotional pain, even if I fail to achieve any particular goal. That is what makes me a whole person and puts me in touch with everyday reality. I want to have the expectation of achievement. Anyone looking at my *curriculum vitae* for employment purposes might well say that I stand no chance of selection. I want to prove to them, and to you, that in many areas I should have as much chance as anyone else — if only people will be open-minded enough to give me the opportunities. I do not want always to have to battle my way through, having to force open doors which have been closed to me. Some people may say that such things are character building, but the constant struggle against attitudes like this has often been more of a cross to bear than my actual disability.

I experienced this kind of negativity right from the early days. I went to see an educational psychologist who labelled me "educationally subnormal" because I would not answer what I considered to be ridiculous questions as to what she was wearing on her wrist and round her neck. That label of "mental retardation" stayed with me for a very long time.

My life at school, when I was five, was extremely hard, due to my poor sight. My reading books had to be written in very large print by hand. There were very few visual aids for partially-sighted children then, and I was always distressed by my inability to cope with blocks of figures. It has been suggested since then that this was probably due to the fact that I could not easily differentiate between columns of work. But if my scholastic achievement was poor, there was even more deprivation in the area of social interaction with my peer group. Mobility was difficult. I used a wheelchair and a tricycle out of doors, while indoors I crawled around the house or other buildings. Here too I was limited by my lack of sight. I had total blindness in the left eye and poor vision in the area of "ten o'clock to four o'clock" in the right eye. How could I possibly get other children to be interested in me?

My salvation came through my Christian faith. I had been brought up on a diet of prayer and regular visits to Sunday School and almost daily readings of the Bible by my mother, so the words of Jesus, and the parables and the imagery within them, were as vivid and as real as any television programme would be today. Jesus was my constant friend when all else seemed to fail. I had a vivid imagination and I could identify with much of his teaching, particularly his way of dealing with the outcasts in the society of his day because I felt 'cast out' by the other children. When they asked me what I had done over the weekend and I told them that I had gone to church, I was frequently laughed at and asked what I had learnt. I would ignore their ridicule and tell some of the scripture stories. I seemed to develop a gift for telling these stories. I related them as though they were real because they felt real to me.

All children like a good story and I quickly became

known for this ability so sometimes they would come and ask me to tell them the stories in the Bible. It was not uncommon for me to have twenty to thirty children surrounding me as I sat on my tricycle in the playground, telling the stories of the Good Samaritan, or the parable of the Sower and many more. So, through my love of Christ, I had been shown a way of communicating God's message, reaching out to others and being accepted by them. Thirty-one years later I was shown that the gift which had been given to me all those years previously was, in fact, a seed that had been planted. It was now about to burst into bloom.

Chapter Three

Towards Healing?

By the age of seven my life was developing into a pattern of regular physiotherapy, combined with various treatments, and endless trips to hospital for one reason or another.

My parents wanted to do all they could for me, and dedicated themselves completely to that cause. Three times a week my mother would take me from our home in East London to Hampstead (in north-west London) for physiotherapy at the Bobath Clinic. My parents committed themselves to giving me two-and-a-half hours of exercises every day. Of course I wanted to be out playing with my friends, but physical improvement had to come first. Both my parents were equally firm about this routine. Sometimes, in those early days, I almost hated them because I was never left alone. Every move, every posture was watched, and often criticised. They did all this for the right reasons, but I felt very resentful about it. I could never satisfy them, or so I felt, and my best never seemed to be good enough. My father's predictable phrase was "It's all right, but you could do better". I do not think I have ever done other than try to please him, but I doubt if I shall ever succeed in doing so. He so wanted me to triumph over my disabilities, and to prove that I was as good as others, but his attitude has caused me much pain over the years — though I do acknowledge that it has probably helped me to get where I am today.

My mother always gave me plenty of encouragement. When I had to master a new skill, she worked unceasingly to help me accomplish it.

The power of prayer was always evident in our home. It was the one constant thing when everything else seemed to be in flux. As a family we believed that faith could "move mountains". We also knew that the power of touch *could* work miracles.

One day in 1957, my mother went to a place in central London to see and hear a famous 'faith-healer'. He seemed to us to be such a spiritual man, and certainly saw himself as a channel for God's work — and some people were healed on the spot. Others just said that they felt better for his touch although they did not know why. All these years later, I know how my contact with people at the door of the church, after my preaching appointments, is as important as the service itself. Contact with other human beings is, in my view, essential because we all need to feel loved and wanted. British "reserve" over touch has been unhelpful to many people. If we look at almost all the examples of Christ ministering the Gospel, we see that most of his miracles of healing — whether of body, mind or spirit — involved touch. I know how vital contact is.

My mother was so impressed with the sensitivity of the healer and his team that she arranged to take me to see him at his sanctuary in the country. I may have been only seven years old, but I was very aware of the tranquillity within the sanctuary there. It had a marvellous sense of peace and stillness. Everyone seemed to matter.

Although many people were present that afternoon, he was never rushed. When he ministered to me he prayed with me and ran his hands down my back. I felt something click into place. From now on, he told my mother, my back would get stronger.

Another member of his team laid her hands over my eyes and I felt a sharp pain surge through them. It may seem ironic now because further damage to my eyes eventually led to total blindness, but from the age of seven to fourteen my sight dramatically improved to the extent that I could read print in the Bible without glasses. Provided I almost put my nose on the paper, I was able to read standard print books. Sadly, at the age of fourteen, I lost my sight altogether but more of that later. All I can say is that after my visit to the sanctuary I was given strength to cope with the many things that were to beset me.

I joined the "prayer for healing" circle and we prayed a certain prayer at the same time each evening. This gave me and my family a great sense of fellowship because we knew that we would be on the prayer chain and therefore had the support of hundreds of other people.

One night, when my mother had put me to bed, I looked

up at the wall in front of me and I could see a deep blue cross almost as though it were illuminated by fluorescent lights, surrounded by a white circle. I called my mother upstairs because I was somewhat frightened by what I had seen. She noticed that there was a second blue cross on the wall over my head. It was not my imagination. Mother and I were obviously tuned in to God's "spiritual force". We wrote to the healer about this and he replied saying that I had been given a very special sign from God and that the power of healing would be made clear in my life.

What do we mean when we speak of 'healing'? For some, it will be miraculous restoration of physical health but, for me, healing can come in many different ways. Healing can be the response by one human being to another in warmth and love and friendship. It can be doing something thoughtful or kindly. Perhaps our Lord does not always want us to receive *physical* healing. Certainly, in my case, I am anything but outwardly whole, yet inwardly I feel a complete person. Knowing that I have received *inner* health and healing, having been given a strength that can only come from God, I feel that God wants me to use my weakness to project His strength to others.

I know that my disability has given me greater compassion. It has enabled me to get alongside other human beings and share their suffering simply because I have had a degree of suffering myself and therefore I can identify with them.

To all intents and purposes I had been anything but healed. I had undergone traumatic surgery on my legs. I was thirteen when I took my first steps. By the time I was fourteen I had become totally blind. Healing indeed!

27

Those three years were devastating and, as a result, I had a nervous breakdown.

How could *I* talk about healing? Yet I am sure that, as the rest of my story unfolds, it will be seen that *inner vision* has a far greater power than physical vision; that in fact my blindness was to bring an even greater fulfilment of God's purpose for me.

Chapter Four

Inner Resources

St John, chapter 9, verses 2 and 3: "Rabbi, who sinned, this man or his parents? Why was he born blind?" "It is not that this man or his parents sinned," Jesus answered, "he was born blind so that God's power might be displayed in curing him" *(New English Bible)*.

I can remember the fateful day as though it were yesterday. I had visited Moorfields Eye Hospital the previous day and had had my usual extensive examination. I could still see the light in my eyes when I came out of the hospital building and thought I was going to have yet another bout of migraine. This was not uncommon due to the strain on my eyes from trying to read small print.

That morning, October 15 1964, I did not go to school due to a severe headache. I lay on the sofa and suddenly noticed a dark shape appear in the right-hand corner of the eye. I was frightened by this and went upstairs to see my mother. She gave me some dark glasses and told me to rest. By the evening the shape had disappeared, but on the following morning I awoke to find that in the house the electric lights had become dark green and outside the sky was bright yellow. The reflected sunlight also made the pavements look a nauseating dark green. I was horrified and screamed out. My parents wanted to take me back to Moorfields but I refused. I said "I was there two days ago. If there had been anything wrong, they would have found it". In the end my parents agreed but said that if it was no better in the morning, they must take me to Moorfields.

By the following day, the symptoms had lessened. My parents kept asking me if I was being honest with them and I assured them that I was. After one week, everything appeared to have returned to normal. I resumed my schooling only to find that gradually I had more and more difficulty in seeing the printed word and reading from the blackboard. As I looked down at my exercise book, it was as though I was looking through a pair of binoculars from the wrong end. Everything was surrounded by a thick black band. I felt sick inside because I knew that the work I was producing was very poor. I frequently had difficulty in reading from the blackboard so it was not uncommon for me to ask classmates to read the text aloud for me.

I was now in Class One, the top class in the school where we had the deputy head, Miss Elsie Chapman, as our form tutor. She was firm but kind. With her we had daily scripture readings and prayers. She was also a very good musician. Every Wednesday morning she took a class in hymn singing. This lesson was my salvation. For almost two years it was the one school activity in which I could fully participate. I knew almost all the hymns from memory — there are still particular ones that strike a strong chord in me, like "Jerusalem" for example, and "Fight the good fight". There was one verse in the latter which was very meaningful to me:

Fight the good fight with all thy might,
Christ is thy strength and Christ thy right;
Lay hold on life and it shall be
Thy joy and crown eternally.

I really did have to "lay hold on life" at this particular time because I felt totally bewildered by what was happening to me. My vision was getting worse day by day, and I had become highly skilled at avoiding either reading anything or trying to find things that had been placed on a table. I would wait until the person went out of the room and feel for the object.

I was afraid to let anyone see what was happening, but inside I was screaming, "Please, somebody help me". The words would get to my throat but would not come out of my mouth. For a period of almost six months, the only person to whom I could confess my fear was the Lord. It was Christ whom I told of my feelings of terror because I knew he would understand and support me. Eventually, however my ordeal came to an end. As was the custom at that time, at the age of 15 I had to undergo a school medical with the (then) London County Council. Part of this medical was an eye test, as were reading and writing. Miss Chapman had shown a great deal of concern about the deterioration of my work and had questioned me on a number of occasions during the previous six months. She wondered whether I was happy at home or whether there might be other family concerns that I wanted to share with her. To all her questions I used a stock answer: "There is absolutely nothing wrong. I am fine". Little did she know!

When I was told about the LCC examination, I made a terrible fuss. A letter was sent home to my mother asking her if she could explain my distress. My mother asked me to read it and had the presence of mind deliberately to give me the letter upside down. Naturally, she was horrified by the realisation that I was seeing very little. We both cried, I with fear, she in sheer distress.

An appointment was made to visit Moorfields the following day. I was examined and then the opthalmic specialist took my parents to one side for a consultation. All I heard was "We will have to have her in". My worst fears were confirmed. Several days later I made my way to Moorfields again to have examinations under anaesthetic. As you can understand, I was terrified. I lay there wondering what would happen to me, and what the final outcome would be. I naturally turned to prayer, as I always did in times of stress. I prayed that all would be well. Please God, no more yellow, no more green. I was thoroughly nauseated by the whole experience. The colours of green and yellow now only occurred in bright sunlight, but I was dazzled by any reflection from white objects. The kitchen and bathroom were the most difficult rooms in the house for me to cope with, just one great blur.

I prayed through much of the night to try and alleviate my anxiety. I summoned up all the resources I had with through my memories of the scriptures. I could identify with the fear that Christ must have felt as he faced his cross, because I knew that this was going to be my cross. Suddenly I had a sense of great peace and stillness because I remembered the words of Christ in the Garden of Gethsemene. "Lord, take this cup away from me," and later, after further prayer, Jesus said "Not my will but thine be done". I could cope if I truly believed it was God's will. I did not know what His purpose was, but I believed that He must have one. If I were to be totally blind I just prayed that God would give me the strength to cope, not for years ahead but one day at a time. I can honestly say that God has totally answered that prayer because the kind of strength I was given can only come from Him, so I went to the operating theatre with trepidation yet knowing I was surrounded by God's love. The outcome was that I had a detached retina in the one eye that I could use and it was detached so severely that it had broken into small fragments. There was no hope. I awoke from the anaesthesia to be told by the doctor, "Well, you'll be blind within three months, so you might as well get used to it". I was too dazed really to care. I think I just said, "Oh, all right". But I was thinking, "What on earth am I going to do now?"

My mother and father had been summoned to see the surgeon. My mother says that she knew what he was going to say but told him she just did not want to know. She told me two years later that she had felt so numb that his words simply did not register. It was something she had always dreaded, as the specialist had told her in my early days that my sight would probably fail. My parents must have questioned why fate had dealt them such a cruel blow. I realised only too clearly that it was nothing that my parents had done. In fact, they could not have been more supportive.

So what was God saying? If we look at the passage from St John's Gospel, chapter 9, where the disciples ask "Rabbi, who sinned, this man or his parents? Why was he born blind?" "It is not that this man or his parents sinned," Jesus answered, "he was born blind so that God's power might be displayed in curing him". God was not pouring down vengeance on my parents, although it might well have felt like that to them. We were victims of circumstance. It just happened. We could either let the experience make us bitter and twisted, or we could try to see how

God's power would be displayed through me.

That could seem a rather arrogant statement on my part. It certainly is not meant to be so. I believe that the concept of inner vision is far more important than physical vision. Effectively, blindness cuts you off from worldly perception, forcing you to draw on inner resources and inner strength. Perhaps one of its greatest attributes is that you have to sense people by their sound. The face can put on a false persona; it can be the image that a person wants to present to the world. But the voice cannot masquerade, it quickly reverts to its original sound. If you listen carefully to any television or radio programme, you will instantly detect insincerity. The voice is the most expressive form of oneself that we have. The atmosphere and aura which surrounds us is felt rather than seen. In just the same way, God's power can be recognised if we allow it to be written in large bold letters upon our hearts and minds.

I hope to show you even more clearly just how Christ has revealed his love, his strength and light in my life as I go on.

Chapter Five

Faith, Music and Literature

In the weeks immediately after the news about my loss of sight, my family and I functioned on "automatic pilot". We were all in a total daze. My younger brother, George, just could not take it in. He would repeatedly write things to see if I could see them. I knew from the tone of his voice that he was becoming more and more alarmed about the situation, and that the realisation of what it meant was finally dawning on him.

My elder brother John's way of dealing with it was to pretend that everything was as it always had been. Nothing was going to stop him doing what he had always done. He would see his girlfriend and go out with his friends, acting as if nothing had happened. He argued that he couldn't *do* anything, so what was the point in "sticking around"? Perhaps, in some way, he was right but John has always done what he wanted to do, regardless of anyone else's feelings or needs! To this day John carries a large chip on his shoulder as a result of the inordinate amount of time Mother had to spend with me, and he has never really come to terms with it.

As a family we had to pick up the pieces of our lives and try to make the best of things. I went back to school and had a very frustrating time. When the other children found out how little I could see, they had a great deal of fun at my expense. They would tell me glass doors were open when they were closed, leave chairs in the middle of the floor for me to fall over, and rub handfuls of mud into my face chanting "Can you see that, Berwick?" These things were bewildering and frightening. I felt more and more angry. I wanted to learn, but did not have the tools to do the job. The only time I could join in was when the lesson involved music of any kind, or scripture. In a scripture class I could not read the text but at least I could take part in the discussions that followed the reading.

I felt as though I would explode with so much confusion and utter bewilderment inside me. My sense of self-esteem was totally destroyed. In fact, it was only when I started to learn Braille that I began to regain some sense of pride in myself. A social worker came once a week to chat and to teach me Braille, writing under the characters so that my mother could also help me each day. Learning to read the dots was extremely frustrating, yet I knew that it was the key to more important things; if I wanted to progress I had no option but to keep working at it.

Learning Braille contractions was the only serious school work I did in almost two years. Things improved a little when I was given a private tutor. She was a considerable help both with reading and with the development of finger dexterity and a good sense of touch. This was achieved by doing basket work and object recognition. You would be surprised at the envy this caused on the part of the other children because cane work was not part of their own school curriculum. I was considered to be the "favourite" and "teacher's pet". This hurt me greatly, but the time was coming when I would be able to walk away from all this, and receive education as a blind person.

A great deal has been written concerning the advantages of integrated education as against special education. Although I approve of the idea of placing disabled children in so-called normal schools, I feel that unless money can be provided to supply the technical equipment that is often required by the disabled pupils, they will be at a distinct disadvantage. If the aim is to have total integration then let us have total commitment on the part of the Education Authorities.

It was important to me that I received an education which was specifically structured for a blind person. I felt that I needed to go into the blind world for a time so that I could adjust to my situation.

It is hard for others to understand the terrible sense of

isolation that one feels when losing one's sight. I felt totally cut off, and needed to learn how others had coped.

Yet another battle ensued to have me educated as a blind person. I had now reached the accepted school-leaving age of sixteen. Moreover, I had thrown the authorities into disarray due to the added difficulty of my multiple handicap. What made things even more problematic was the fact that these disabilities had not rendered me educationally sub-normal. If they had, I would have been placed without any difficulty.

The end of the school holidays in September 1966 found me waiting, as usual, for the school bus. To our amazement it drove straight past the front door. My mother telephoned the school to find out what had happened. She was told by the headmistress that I had left school in July. We could not believe it! How could they do such a thing without any kind of consultation or discussion as to my future? I felt as if nobody cared about me. I was just one big problem and a burden to the people I loved. There had to be a reason for all this. What was God trying to say?

The words of Psalm 23 kept coming to me: "Yea, though I walk through the valley of the shadow of death, I will fear no evil, for thou are with me". It might not have been the shadow of death but it certainly seemed a very dark and frightening valley. My world had been turned upside down and, except for my parents, no-one seemed interested. It made me feel that if I ever got through all this, I would strive to succeed and make people sit up and take notice of me.

The cards were stacked against me. I had only been able to walk for two years — and that was thanks to the surgery which had been carried out on my legs. Now I was afraid to move.

I felt extremely angry at the attitude of the head-mistress. One of her best friends worked with blind and partially-sighted children, but no help of understanding was forthcoming. My parents took up the challenge of my education. They were determined that I was not going to be dumped on the scrap heap.

My social worker started negotiating with various school and eventually an interview was secured at Dorton House. My days there have been well-documented in *Undefeated,* my first book, but I think I need to cover here some of the problems, issues and feelings that arose from my first experience of boarding school.

My initial feeling was that here was a great opportunity to work hard and gain confidence in myself. This proved to be true. It was my stay at Dorton House that shaped me into the person I am today. Boarding school forced me to separate from my mother, who always provided me with a loving, secure environment. For the first time in my life I had to stand on my own two feet, metaphorically speaking, because in reality I was the first physically disabled student to be accepted at Dorton House.

The original school building was certainly not suitable for someone in a wheelchair. One of its main features was a wide sweeping staircase such as you would find in a stately home or on the film set for a gala ball or royal occasion. I can remember that it took me some fifteen minutes to walk up the forty stairs to my dormitory.

The support I needed, and received, from the staff triggered off feelings of jealousy in other pupils who, because of their visual handicap, were unaware of my limitations, believing me to be attention-seeking. They had no idea of my walking posture and the terrific struggle that was involved in going upstairs, getting in and out of bed, getting dressed. Yet again my physical disability put me out on a limb, through no fault of my own. However, I knew that no matter how much I felt out of things, this was a "make or break" situation for me. For the first time I had it within my grasp to show people that I was capable of making something of my life, and I would not give up on this until I had accomplished it.

At Dorton House I received an immense broadening of my experience, both academic and spiritual. My most vivid memory is of my first working day, when I entered the hall for morning assembly. There to greet me was the sound of a lovely old pipe organ, expertly played by the blind music master, Michael Campbell. It was music to my ears! If that were the sign of things to come, then I was glad that I found myself in this place. No more would I be going through the motions of learning. This was the real thing!

It was wonderful to handle a hymn book once again, although I found it impossible to keep up with the other pupils. It's one thing learning the Braille system, yet another to identify the dots on the page. The staff were extremely encouraging to me. They thought I had done well to learn all the Braille characters. I never felt at any time that they were irritated by my slowness. On the contrary, it was I who became angry. I suppose I wanted to run before I could walk. After all, I was on a six-weeks trial period, so I had to prove myself.

My mind was in a spin, trying to cope with this new way of life, and yet I was enjoying the challenge. Especially good were the English literature lessons. Shakespeare, Brontë, George Elliot, Kipling, Tolstoy, Fleming and so many others — the world of classical literature was really opening up before me, and it was an exciting discovery. I devoured all that came my way. In some ways this experience was spiritual, because of the power of the English language. I soaked it up like a sponge.

Music was another way of tapping my emotions. It was this that was the deciding factor in my sense of well-being at Dorton House. Flute lessons with Michael Campbell and the chance of singing in a well-trained choir were wonderful. It was fantastic to drink in all this marvellous music and not to be regarded as odd or "posh" as I had been in my East London school.

I should like to say "Thank you" to the staff at Dorton House for giving me that vital education. I have never tired of learning and, over the years, frequent visits to concerts, listening to records and now compact discs have given me immense pleasure. Music is like that well-known brand of lager; it reaches the parts others cannot reach. I feel very close to God when listening to the Fauré Requiem, Mozart's violin concertos or the Sibelius cello concerto, and I love the mood changes of Beethoven. For me, Beethoven is colour in sound, with infinite variations of light and shade.

The religious knowledge lessons were great! I had got my hands on a bible again, even though I was struggling like mad to read it. Those people who are fortunate enough to have normal sight probably rarely give a second thought to the fact that they can pick up a book or newspaper and read it! The ability to read is a very precious, God-given gift that one does not appreciate until one no longer has it. Mail can be the most difficult problem. You have no way of knowing what is in the envelope, so whom do you select to read it? Can you know that it will be read in confidence? Today there are machines that will read printed matter in a synthesized speech but, at the time of writing, they cost £10,000. This is well beyond the reach of most blind people unless they are employed and can have the equipment on a permanent loan basis from the Disabled Advisory Service (a government-funded agency) or can persuade one of the grant-making trusts to purchase it for them. I believe that every blind person has the right to have the opportunity of reading the printed word.

Religious studies were enhanced by using the commentaries by William Barclay and J.B. Phillips. Our tutor, Margaret Bolton, was steeped in her subject, making the Bible and its issues come alive. In fact, I would go so far as to say that it was she who helped me along the path to becoming a preacher.

I can see how the concept of the Trinity could be applied in my development. When we think of the three faces of God, we think of God the Father, God the Son and God the Holy Spirit. I know that God cannot be compartmentalised in that way, it is merely man's inadequate way of describing a powerful spiritual force. My three-fold aspect is composed of faith, music and literature. These three have been responsible for my spiritual maturing. Deprivation of any one of them would have stunted my spiritual growth.

I have never worked so hard in my life as I did during that six-week trial period at Dorton House. People were so kind, yet also quite tough. The staff were obviously told to give me a full assessment and they certainly did! I stuck this for almost the whole of the six weeks, then one night the strain got to me. It was during "prep". I was struggling with the Braille when suddenly I started to cry. One of the pupils went and called the member of staff who was on duty. It happened to be Joan Brown, the deputy head. She was particularly understanding, leading me away from other members of the class.

We talked of many things through my tears. I repeatedly apologised for being so stupid. She assured me that I was not stupid, that I had done very well. The tears had been expected, it had only been a question of when. It was the first time I had wept over the loss of my sight. I told her that I wanted to stay at the school but the pressure of not knowing whether I would be accepted, on top of everything else, was very difficult to cope with. She said that she would ask Mr Bolton, the Headmaster, to tell me his decision in the morning. His decision was that I could stay! Now I could really get down to serious learning.

I suppose the greatest tribute to my efforts was paid by Jill Smith, when I went back to an old pupils' reunion some years ago. She introduced me to the new headmaster and said "This is our Superwoman". I laughed, and she said it had never been known in the history of the school to have a pupil move from learning Braille to passing 'O' levels and a flute examination in just eighteen months. I think my success opened a door, because they now take quite a number of multipli-disabled children. Dorton House now has a new school building and accommodation block that has been purpose-built for pupils who use a wheelchair.

Chapter Six

Training for the big wide World

I had left the security of Dorton House. School life was over and a new phase of my life was about to begin. I was eighteen years old, had my 'O' level certificates and had begun to believe in my own ability. I did not have to convince myself of that, but I had to prove it to others. I was determined that I would succeed in that big outside world, but first it would be necessary for me to go to Heatherset, the Vocational Training Assessment Unit in Surrey.

In 1969 few job opportunities existed for the blind, still fewer for a blind person with a physical handicap. The type of employment available was only too predictable unless one was academically inclined. Outside academia, the only options were light assembly work, secretarial duties or telephony. The easy way out for me would have been to accept placement in a factory doing very basic assembly work. I had other ideas! Although none of these options really appealed to me, I decided to put to good use the gifts of perfect speech and hearing that the good Lord had given me. I decided to become a telephonist. The most important consideration was that the work be sedentary.

I knew I could not manage the old-fashioned "dolls eye" switchboard as my hands went into too much spasm trying to find the correct slots and push the plugs in, but I had been shown a modern "PABX 1" switchboard on a day's visit to Pembridge Place, the commercial training college in London run by the Royal National Institute for the Blind. I knew that this was well within my capabilities but I had to convince the authorities of this. It was a task that proved to be enormously difficult. None of the officials believed that it would be possible. Light assembly work appeared to be the answer, so why look elsewhere? Nevertheless, I stuck out for what I believed in, and would not accept their other suggestions until I had explored every possible avenue to becoming a telephonist. After many weeks of struggling against adverse opinion, a dummy switchboard was brought to the vocational training centre for me to get what is now called "hands on" experience. Much to the officials' surprise I could, as I had claimed many times, operate this board with no problem whatever. The board had been modified for a blind operator by removing the flashing lights and putting in an electric solanoid which produced a pulsating tactile indicator where the light had been situated. I applied for a place at Pembridge Place training college and waited to see if I would be given it. It was still hard for the powers-that-be to imagine that any employer would treat my aspiration seriously. The reality was that it was not the job market that held me back — on the whole, employers have been quite good. It was the RNIB which was the toughest nut to crack. At that time they had dealt with very few multipli-disabled but intelligent people who were capable of holding down a job in a competitive market. I was determined that I would become the exception rather than the rule.

Almost two years passed before my chance came. The telephony tutor refused to teach me because she said that she was paid to teach the blind, not spastics. Thankfully, twenty years on, we are more enlightened. Due to the pressure put on her by various bodies to change her views, she resigned at the end of 1969 and by January 1970 I was given that much-desired place.

I can never understand why the various charities will not unite to help a person with the specific needs resulting from multiple disability. St Dunstan's, the society to assist war-blinded people, is a good example. They have the expertise and the knowledge to help someone who has difficulty with their hands in addition to being blind, but they cannot do so because their constitution states that they may only assist those persons who are war-blinded. It is good to see charities beginning to work much more closely together now. Although fewer disabled babies are born today, those who are often suffer from multiple disability and that frequently requires the co-operation of a number of charitable institutions.

During the long wait for a place, I had to keep my mind alert. I did this by helping my parents with their work for the East London Spastic Society. As a family, we had been associated with it since 1954. My father had held various offices there, as transport officer, treasurer and now secretary. Since the inception of the society, it had been the members' ambition to have their own centre. The original concept was that of a treatment centre, but this was later revised as physiotherapy had become much more readily available under the national Health Service. The great need now was a place for social activities. Our family became very involved with many fund-raising projects for this purpose. It took from 1954 until the early 1970s for that ambition to be realised. All through my childhood, it seemed, I had been involved in some way with charity work. No wonder I was to take up the challenge myself some years later.

My parents worked very hard for the cause – Dad on various committees, and Mum doing vital practical tasks such as preparation of food for social events. When the Centre opened, she ran the bar. She had a great talent with people, and could quite easily cope with their many speech problems or shaky limbs.

I know that Dad was very proud of the Centre — he had supervised and been responsible for tendering much of the work. To keep costs down he had done much of the renovating and building work himself. I can remember that we hardly ever had a meal in peace at that time without the phone ringing or someone calling about the Centre. Mum was pretty good about it all. I suppose you could say the end justified the means!

When I think of what the original building was like, I realise we achieved a real transformation. It had been a disused yoghourt warehouse. Trees were growing in what once had been the freezer section of the warehouse! Dad and other members of the committee themselves cut down the trees and cleared the site and, after many months of work, the Centre looked most attractive. A stage replaced the old freezer section. It was a great day when the East London Spastic Society Centre (at 327 Newham Way, East Ham, London E6) was officially opened by the well-known boxer, Henry Cooper.

During this waiting period for a place at Pembridge Place, I became involved in other aspects of the work of the Spastic Society itself. The Committee was largely made up of a group of well-meaning parents who thought that their disabled offspring were still children, and the entertainment they provided largely reflected that view. The majority of members were either middle-aged or in their late teens and early twenties. The "recipients" would complain, saying that they were fed up with being treated like children, they wanted to get out and see more of life. I was elected as their spokeswoman to articulate their views at the various committee meetings. As a result, at the annual general meeting of 1969, I was asked by the society if I would form a club for those spastics who were over the age of sixteen. I said that I would, but only on condition that such a club should be open to people with other disabling conditions as well as cerebral palsy and to the able-bodied too. In this way, I believed, greater integration would be achieved. This idea generated a great deal of opposition, not only at that meeting but for many years to come.

The East London Spastic and Handicapped Club, later to be known as the Disabled Fellowship Club of East London, was formed with the aid of a £50 grant from the Spastic Society on July 18 1969. I quickly realised that one of our biggest problems was going to be suitably-adapted transport for the members. In the early days we hired almost anything that had four wheels and an engine, plus two willing helpers to lift people in and out, but I knew that this would not be a permanent solution. Someone would eventually be injured as a result of such unsuitable transport. So I set about raising funds for a hydraulic tail-gate ambulance. Committee members of the Spastic Society thought the idea ludicrous and fanciful. They said that I would have to be content with a ramped vehicle, but I refused this option because of the dangers of busy London streets, so packed with cars that there was little space for lowering the ramp. The other consideration was the safety of both the helper and the member. Then, in January 1970, I started at Pembridge Place and for a time had to put aside my ideas for the ambulance.

I was terrified that first morning at Pembridge Place, when I realised what confronted me. The college consisted of two old buildings knocked into one, with a narrow walkway between them and flights of difficult stairs with fire doors immediately at the top of them. There were very narrow corridors between classrooms that were cluttered with pieces of equipment. The college Principal had stated that I was to be escorted at all times throughout the course as his staff was not prepared to assist or take responsibility for me.

During the first week I had helpers from the British Red Cross Society. These helpers had great difficulty in coping, so eventually my mother took on the role of attendant. It was decided that because of my disability and the problems relating to the structure of the building, I would have to complete my training within three months. Other students took six to twelve months. There were certainly no concessions for my additional problems. It was tremendously hard work — even my mother says that she did not know how I stood the pace. One of the tasks was to memorise five hundred STD codes, another was to be able to recall six London telephone numbers. The tutor gave me these in a block and then requested that I recite these back to him at random as well as knowing the order in which he had given them to me. Braille had to be written accurately at twenty-six words a minute, and read accurately at a minimum of forty-six words a minute. Telephone numbers had to be noted at a speed of not less than eighteen a minute. The Braille directory of useful telephone numbers that we created had to be dot-perfect. One single error meant that the whole page was torn up and re-worked. Another test was to see how many calls I could answer in a given space of time, and to see how agitated I would become if abused by a caller. Any negative response on my part would have meant failure to complete the course. As the end of the three months I had passed, with distinction, the Telephony Training College Course and now had to go out into the big wide world to take my chances there. I just prayed that God would help me in this new venture and trusted that all would be well.

Chapter Seven

"Does he take sugar?"

Finding a job proved more difficult than I had anticipated, but I was determined than I was not going to give up. The Disablement Resettlement Officer was well-meaning, but I do think he approached the task of securing me a position with an in-built defeatism. My way of dealing with this problem was to contact his office several times a week and become a thorn in his side!

I also took this line with the employment officer of the Royal National Institute for the Blind. Here was one student they would not be allowed to forget in a hurry! I soon discovered that phone calls were not the answer — they could easily be forgotten — but letters had to be filed! The other lesson I quickly learned was not to sit back waiting for something to happen, but to get on and see what I could find out for myself.

Months went by during which I did not have much success. In fact, as soon as prospective employers heard of my multiple disability, they quickly became disinterested. I was almost beginning to wonder if I should tell them about it or not; if I simply turned up for the appointed interview, the person concerned would have no preconceived ideas about my limitations. I knew that there were quite a number of people who took that approach, but I did not feel that it was quite fair. Additionally, I would be in a position of not being able to find out details about access to and within the building and, even worse, could have given the impression that I had set out to deceive my prospective employer.

One day my mother was reading the job advertisements in the paper when she came across a post for a senior telephonist in a city bank. It was for the kind of switchboard I could manage, so I would be able to do the job if only they would agree to adapt the switchboard for a blind operator. I rang and was given an appointment. I then contacted the Disablement Resettlement Officer who in turn contacted the bank.

I was absolutely terrified on the morning of the interview. It was pouring with rain which added to my already slow progress into the building. I was also trying to protect my Braille books and shorthand Braille writer from the downpour. The accountant who was to interview me had requested that I bring them along so that he could see how I proposed to do the work. As I entered the Commonwealth Trading Bank of Australia (later known as the Commonwealth Bank of Australia), the accountant who came to meet me said "I didn't realise you would be so disabled, but you might as well sit down anyway".

July 14th 1970, which I had so eagerly anticipated, had begun to feel like a day of disaster. Ultimately, Mr Chandler turned out to be a very good friend to me but that interview got off to a bad start. Like so many people, he had preconceived ideas about certain aspects of disability. He was a very kind, Christian man who had done a great deal of work in his local Leonard Cheshire Home. To Mr Chandler, to be cerebral palsied included a speech impediment. He proceeded to conduct the interview on that basis by addressing all the questions to my mother.

It is an attitude which is known to the disabled as "Does he take sugar?". It is also an attitude which makes me very angry. I do not know why this is — perhaps it is fear or embarrassment, but it does seem that disability automatically creates that sort of attitude. People talk as though you were not there or, worse still, treat you as a child. Both are deeply humiliating. On this occasion I was going red in the face while my mother was nudging me under the table, telling me (through clenched teeth) to keep quiet. Eventually she found herself saying, "Look, it was not me who trained as a telephonist. Why don't you ask my daughter?". To his enormous credit, Mr Chandler immediately apologised and said "I thought that, being spastic, you would have a speech impediment". I replied "Well, sir, I'd hardly be applying for the post of senior telephonist if I couldn't speak". Mr Chandler took my point immediately and said "Let's begin the interview all over again, shall we?" We did, and this time my mother was totally ignored.

Some may feel that I am being unfair in mentioning this incident, but I use it as an illustration that shows how easy it is for people to fall into this trap. The disabled are individual people, and their particular disability is unique to them. No two people experience a disabling condition in the same way. To generalise is dangerous. What we need to do is to build bridges of understanding, to create empathy but not induce pity. I wanted to be treated on equal terms and, apart from that first misunderstanding, in that organisation I was.

The interview seemed to be going quite well, though naturally my safety and general mobility around the building were of paramount importance. Mr Chandler escorted my mother through all the areas that I would have to negotiate each day, while I went into the switchboard room to meet the operator and listen to what went on. While I was there, the operator was asked to make a call to Australia — it sounded as though the job could be quite interesting. A call to Australia is, in reality, no different from any other call, but when so much hangs in the balance it all seems exciting and just a little daunting.

After some time, June (the operator) asked me if I would like a turn. I said that I would but that she would have to tell me which lights were flashing as the board had not yet been adapted for a blind operator. This she duly did, and I put my whole self into it. Although I had not realised it, Mr Chandler had crept silently into the room and was listening to my technique. He congratulated me and said he was very impressed with what he had heard. He invited me back into his office for a further chat. I felt I was in with a chance! I just had to keep on trying to create a good impression. If I didn't believe in myself, no one else would. I made a suggestion that surprised him. "Sir," I said, "if you will give me a month's trial, I'll work for that time without pay. In that way your company won't have lost out, but I will have gained valuable work experience." He was amazed by my suggestion but I could tell that it had pleased him. He said he would think things over. Well, it was a start; at least I had not received the outright rejection I had anticipated. The employment officer of the RNIB turned up too late for the interview, but Mum said that she could see him pleading my case through the glass window of Mr Chandler's office. I had done my best, and it was now a matter of praying that all would be well.

My prayers were answered, for the next morning Mr Chandler rang my mother. "I'm going to give that girl a chance," he said, "she's got guts." Mum could hardly speak for emotion and when she passed the call over to me I wasn't much better. There was certainly great joy that day in our household. Outside, Mum told almost everyone we met. I was amazed by the attitude of the neighbours down our street, however. Instead of joy, there was almost

51

incredulity that I would be earning £16 a week, a good wage in 1970. I suppose they had assumed I would go to some kind of occupational centre and earn a mere pittance for my efforts. But I knew I was on my way to a better life and I prayed that no more obstacles would be put in my way.

I was due to start work on August 17th. I had a holiday with my parents, although it was hard to relax because all I could think about was making a success of the job. I had been given a list of more than 250 staff members and their departments which I committed to memory. I knew absolutely nothing about banking, but I decided that I could at least learn some of the terminology that was used. I reasoned that everything else would sort itself out in God's good time. I couldn't wait for that first morning.

When it came, things went very badly for me. I wanted to make a good impression but I was let down by the taxi which turned up late to take me there. Then, to my utter dismay, I found that the switchboard had not been adapted. I just could not believe it! I was going to lose this job through no fault of my own. Everything and everybody seemed to be against me. All I could do was pray. Those prayers were answered. Mr Chandler could not have been more understanding. Within a day of my arrival the switchboard was adapted, and within four days I was told that I could keep the job.

Six weeks later, Mr Chandler came and asked me if I knew anyone who would like a job in the post room. I said, "Yes, my mother. Phone her up and see if she's interested". This would be another answer to prayer as far as I was concerned. For fifteen years mother had worked on a sewing-machine at home, earning a meagre wage and working long, lonely hours. When I look back,

I do not know how she did it. Running a home, taking me back and forth to hospital and completing a given quota of work — she was a marvel. I so wanted to take her out of this situation. She was becoming more and more withdrawn through spending so much time on her own and with so little opportunity to socialise. Being in the bank, she would have the opportunity of meeting people and becoming a person in her own right.

Mother accepted the job. It proved, in fact, to be a very shrewd move on Mr Chandler's part. He now had someone who knew better than anyone else how to help me. She was there to guide me around the building, to be with me at meal times and minister to any needs I might have. This freed other members of staff from having to give me assistance. Although this was a great help, it did change my relationship with my work colleagues. They left it all to Mum and, although we made joint friends, only two ever became close to me individually. I somehow lived my life through my mother, and it was to her that they went if they had things that concerned me personally, such as wage slips or bank statements, or even faults with their telephones. This made me feel very angry indeed. Our roles were reversed some thirteen years later, when I spoke for my mother at our joint leaving presentation.

Apart from this, the bank was extremely good to me, allowing time off for medical reasons, study and social service work for the disabled. They were involved in fund-raising schemes for the ambulance for the East London Spastic and Handicapped Club, permitting a raffle once a fortnight when we were paid. This was organised by Mr Sydney Crook, a member of staff who was later to become my transport officer, and his wife Helen. They worked unceasingly, helping me with many projects for the Club.

The bank, and Mr Chandler (sadly, now deceased) in particular, played a key role in helping me to get a bank loan so that I could help my parents put down a deposit towards the purchase of our council home in Poplar, East London.

I can see now how all these events were part of God's rich pattern. Things could not have worked out better if I had planned events for myself. Working at the bank gave me the security I needed and, even after my retirement, the opportunity of taking full advantage of the special concessions they offered to members of staff, such as a preferential mortgage rate, were given to me. Some may say that these were just the perks of the job. I do not see it in that way. I see it as God richly blessing me and providing me with a real quality of life. For that, I am ever thankful.

Chapter Eight

Towards a new Life

I settled down at the bank very well. In 1970, I was awarded a Braille watch by the American Embassy for perseverance in overcoming the difficulties related to my disability. Sixteen thousand blind people were eligible. Of these, only six women and six men would be awarded a Braille watch. I was given one for the way I had coped at the Commercial Training College. I was amazed. I did not think I had done anything worthy of an award. It was good, however, to visit the American Embassy and meet the Ambassador, Mr W.E. Weld. This was a happy interlude before the problems which were to develop later.

I had started to have very severe pain in both my eyes. There was a feeling of great pressure over the eyes and across the nose, and I was also experiencing terrible headaches. Eventually I reached the stage where I could hardly hold my head up. Leaning over the switchboard and answering calls in a cheerful voice while in such intense pain was anything but easy.

During this period the taxi which took me to work was repeatedly late. One day I was called into Mr Chandler's office where he stated that unless I could 'sort this problem out', I would be in danger of losing my job. Naturally I was very worried and the anxiety which this caused me exacerbated the pain in my eyes. I talked it over with my parents, and Dad said he could not sit back and see me lose the job I had fought so hard to obtain, because of travelling difficulties. He said he would give up his job in the building trade and see if he could get a job in the city. As luck would have it, he did eventually achieve this. He took a position as a messenger in a bank near the one in which I was employed. This meant that he could take me to work. This change also benefited him because he now had job security during the winter months and that he certainly had not had in the building trade. We now all travelled to work together and that was a great blessing. I know it was all part of God's rich pattern. He had provided for me and my family most handsomely.

Although the problem of getting to work had been resolved, the difficulties with my eyes did not improve. The problem became so severe that I just had to admit defeat. I rang Moorfields Eye Hospital to make an appointment. Dad just could not believe I had done so. He knew that I must be desperate because I had had such an aversion to that place since my experience there in 1965 when I lost my sight.

Mum, Dad and I made our way to casualty. I knew that things were far from good and this was confirmed by the doctor on duty. Within minutes he summoned a senior consultant who examined me with care and concentration. "What have you been doing lately?" he asked. "Going to work," I replied, "playing the flute, teaching the children, nothing much." "There is no more flute-playing, ever again," he said. "You have glaucoma, and the level is dangerously high. You should have been flat on your back some time ago. I don't know how you've managed to work with the pain." To be honest, I did not know either. There then followed a series of treatments with steroids, drugs to counteract the effects of the steroids, antibiotics, and cortisone to help with the pain, plus artificial tears to lubricate the eyes. All this was to last for eight years. My general health slowly deteriorated as a result of these treatments, but I was determined to keep going.

I had one compensation. It was the enjoyment I received from the fund-raising I did for the Ambulance. We were inching towards the total, but it was quite difficult. We had large donations from Top Ten Promotion, from the Worshipful Company of Drapers and from the Worshipful Company of Cutlers. The fund-raising that we were able to do ourselves was pretty low-key, but small donations are, nevertheless, vital to the general running of smaller charities. Sadly, with changes in government policy, there are increasing demands made of grant-making organisations and I think myself that charitable resources will be stretched to such an extent that they may become ineffective.

The day that the Ambulance was officially handed over was a great occasion. I felt that this was a personal victory for me, because a lot of critics within the Society had said that it would be impossible to realise this ambition. They had also said that the hydraulic lift on the ambulance was unnecessary. My view, however, was validated when a year later they applied for and received a "Sunshine Coach" from the Variety Club of Great Britain which had the identical tail-gate hydraulic lift for wheelchairs.

In 1973 I was awarded the Spastics Society "Achievement of the Year Award". That gave me and the Club a great deal of publicity which was good news for our work, but it never ceases to amaze me how critical some people are of media coverage if they are not involved themselves. I realise that each and every person working for the cause deserved equal credit, but the fact was that it was *my* unique circumstances that made the impact on the media. If my own multiple disability can be used to help others then, for me, all the problems that I have faced in my life have been worthwhile.

All this publicity was well-received by the bank. The London office really was "put on the map". Features appeared in the bank's journal, *Bank Notes,* which was issued to all its branches, most of which were in Australia. I was featured four times in *Bank Notes* in thirteen years — an extremely rare event. The bank was marvellous about all this, co-operating by giving me time off to attend various functions. They regarded it, I am sure, as good public relations.

When the Ambulance was handed over, I was overjoyed. Once again, my prayers had been answered. It was commented by some people that I would not be happy until the club owned "a fleet of these things". They were right! More vehicles would mean an increased membership because we would be providing people with what they needed. The committee worked tremendously hard to give the members a good quality of social life. Almost every week the ambulance was used for a trip to a concert, theatre, or some other place of interest. If funds permitted, we went to a restaurant for a meal. That may seem an odd thing to provide, but I felt this would greatly help to boost people's confidence. Many of our people had never eaten out in public so this was a special challenge to those who had difficulties with eating. All too often they had not put themselves in this situation for fear of embarrassing other customers, or worse still, of being refused entry by the restaurant manager. My argument was that they had as much right to be there as anyone else. My committee fortunately was of the same mind.

We were also ably assisted with our work by a team of policemen from Hornchurch who drove the ambulances and gave general help as required. There was a second ambulance in 1976, thanks to a broadcast on "Capital Radio" where various articles were auctioned to raise funds, and many local public houses donated money to help us reach our target. The broadcaster, Joan Shenton, captured the imagination of the public with the appeals that she made with Tommy Vance on their morning show. This gave us a high profile which in turn increased our membership and raised a large percentage of the money required. When we broke away from the East London Spastics Society as a result of the disagreement over the issue of welcoming people with disabilities other than cerebral palsy, we invited Joan and Tommy to become our Vice Presidents.

The late Andrew Cruickshank willingly agreed to become our President. I had met Andrew several years before and he became more and more interested in the work. Wherever possible, he attended major functions or fund-raising events. His friendship had a great influence on me. It was Andrew who later advised me to write my first book (which was called *Undefeated*). I submitted every chapter to him; he made comments, gave encouragement, and generally showed a great deal of interest.

There was much to do now that we had broken away and become a registered charity in our own right. "The Disabled Fellowship Club of East London", as it had now become, was at last free to make its own decisions. It had taken six years for us to reach that stage, but it was worth it. My life seemed to be almost taken over by the club and its activities, but thankfully not entirely.

Just one year previously I had made two decisions that were to alter the direction of my life completely and, because of these, I was to change my career and ultimately build a new life for myself. God clearly revealed to me the path he wanted me to take.

Grateful though I was for the job at the bank, I wanted something more from life. I knew that I could put my brain to greater use. I felt as though I was stagnating and I knew I must find a way out. But how?

For my confirmation in the Anglican Church I had undergone a period of intense study. I felt deeply privileged to learn that I would be confirmed by Bishop Trevor Huddleston, Bishop of Stepney. He was someone I admired because of his stance on South Africa.

I was 25 years old when I was confirmed. Family and friends gathered at St Matthias Church, Poplar, for this special occasion. The Rev Christopher Idle had been

59

especially helpful to me in preparing for this great day, putting biblical texts on tape, and reading any other theological material that he felt I might find helpful or interesting. I know he was really proud that I had made this commitment. I had thought the whole thing through very carefully, knowing only too well what a serious undertaking it was. Here was the time when I would stand up and publicly proclaim my love for the Lord and my total obedience to serving him. That is why, when it was assumed that I would be wheeled to the altar, I said that I wanted to walk so long as people did not mind my slowness. Bishop Huddleston said that he did not mind in the least; this was something worth waiting for. When I walked forward, I felt that I was the only person in that building, although in reality it was almost full. When the Bishop laid his hands on my head and said, "Confirm, O Lord, Thy servant Linda", the tears welled up inside me because I knew that the thing I most wanted to do in life was to serve God. I felt an enormous sense of peace and stillness, and in that moment of quietness I prayed to God to show me what He wanted me to do with my life. That day I received my answer. I must do something where I would show God's compassion for others. I was trying to show God's compassion to other disabled people through my work in the Club, but I knew that was not all that God wanted. He was asking more of me. I could not think what it could be so I prayed that He would reveal it to me.

I soon had my answer. I knew I had to work in one of the caring professions.

I had applied for training in social work but had been told that it would not be possible for me because in this field one has to do what are known as 'placements'. This would necessitate working in a hospital, home, probation office or some similar place, and I would obviously be too much of a liability. All I could do was to keep on praying that God would show me the way forward, and one day He certainly did! It came in a most unusual way, and yet when I think about it, it was in one of the most logical ways — through the radio. I was listening to a programme on BBC Radio Four called "If you think you've got problems" introduced by Jean Metcalf, with Dr James Hemming and Dr Wendy Greengross. It was a programme in which people could discuss their problems with Dr Hemming and Dr Greengross, and the discussions were carried out in a very quiet and informed way. The person would be encouraged to reason things out in their own mind, often discovering their own solutions to the problems. I was struck by how brave those people were in opening up to complete strangers, yet I realised that this was where the advantage lay. You cannot always talk easily and frankly to family or friends. So this was Counselling! I listened, fascinated. Several weeks went by and the more I listened to this programme the more an ideal formulated in my mind. Here was a job I could do, provided I was psychologically suitable. I would be seated, and as the client would come to me the question of mobility would not arise. I had a good brain, good hearing and, as I have said earlier, I also had perfect speech which is relatively rare for people who have cerebral palsy. This gift of perfect speech was God-given and I felt therefore that I must use it. The more I prayed about it, the more I knew it was right. I contacted the BBC and asked to speak to Dr Greengross. I was told that it would not be possible for me to talk to her but, if I would write, they would see that she got my letter.

You have probably gathered by now that when I make up my mind I have to act upon it there and then, especially when I know something is so right for me! I knew that

Wendy had a London practice, so I asked directory enquiries for the number. Instead of the number being of the practice, it turned out to be her home number. Wendy, being the wonderful person that she is, did not send me off "with a flea in my ear", but listened to what I had to say. At the end of our conversation I felt as though we had known each other for years, and thankfully she promised to give me all the help she could in finding out about training.

Eventually I was accepted on an introductory course one evening a week at Westminster Pastoral Foundation (then in Central Hall, Westminster). It was quite a small organisation at that time, but one really had a sense that people genuinely cared. It was a Christian organisation, founded by a Methodist clergyman. Because of the way in which this organisation reached out to the community, I began to see how Methodism appealed to my social conscience.

On this introductory course I discovered that it was in the compassionate aspect of counselling that I felt I could see Christ's love in action. The lines of the hymn

Lord, thy church on earth is seeking
Thy renewal from above;
Teach us all the art of speaking
With the accent of thy love.

seemed to me to epitomise the purpose of counselling. This training is one of the things that set me on the path to becoming a Methodist Local Preacher.

If you are to undergo serious counselling training, one of the requirements is that you must have personal therapy or psychoanalysis. So I set to work in earnest and began what turned out to be a four-year commitment to personal therapy. I now had everything to look forward to. I was where I wanted to be, I was going to make the most of it and really dedicate myself to the work.

I loved every minute of the course. It was all very fascinating and stretched the mind wonderfully. It was totally different from anything the average person from the East End would normally have expected to study although, thirteen years on, that has now changed. Because of the high cost of training fees, professional counselling and psychotherapy have, in the past, tended to be middle-class professions.

The philosophy of counselling was very difficult for my parents to understand. They believed that what went on in the privacy of the home was one's own problem and no-one else's. They thought that feelings and views should only be expressed within the family and to do anything else was to betray family loyalties. In their opinion nothing could be achieved by talking to a complete stranger about personal or family affairs. Consequently the concept of complete confidentiality was hard for them to understand. Often when they asked me about the things we talked about in my therapy, I would say "Oh, this and that". Thus I came to be regarded as secretive and disloyal, particularly if we had had a difference of opinion during the previous week. I am sure this sense of rejection is often felt, to a greater or lesser degree, by the partners or parents of someone who undertakes counselling training. Nevertheless I was prepared to stick it out. It was something I believed in and I knew that, eventually, they would get used to the idea that this was all part of the job, as indeed they did. However, I was to receive another blow to my confidence before the training really got under way.

The pain in my eyes worsened. Then, one day in the bank, after taking the lift to the second floor, I slipped on the marble floor. Someone had spilt some tea and the rubbers on my tripod sticks found it. (Tripods on a wet floor are very dangerous — it is impossible to balance.) I fell to the ground with a heavy thud, hitting my head on the ground. Mum, who just a few seconds earlier had walked forward to open the swing doors, was powerless to save me. I can remember saying "For God's sake, don't move me". I had a really sharp pain across my eyes. After a little while, I got to my feet, feeling dazed but all right. I found out later that this bang on the head had increased the pressure behind the eye, causing it to burst. The pain in my eyes grew more and more intense, and three weeks later the hospital consultant said that my left eye would have to be removed. I felt terrified by the idea. How would it look? And how would I feel? Actually, when the prosthesis is in the eye socket, I don't *feel* any different (in fact, it's much better looking than the original), but when the artificial eye is removed, I hate it! I don't like the feeling as the eyelid drops into the empty space. It is at times like this that I hate my body. The operation was simple and, apart from some horrible side effects from some drugs which did not mix, it was comparatively easy.

While I was a patient in Moorfields, I was asked if I would visit the hospital radio station and be interviewed by one of their presenters. It was felt that my story might inspire people who were struggling to come to terms with defective sight. I gladly did this, and spent a very happy evening in the studio talking to the patients and choosing my favourite pieces of music. I suppose you could say it was the ordinary man or woman's *Desert Island Discs*. The station controller liked my style and asked me if I would like to have my own programme. I eagerly agreed as I loved anything to do with broadcasting. So after leaving hospital, I returned once a week to do my programme. First I acted as co-presenter with Hugh Vale, and the programme was called *The L + H Hour*. Later I had my own programme called *Lin Berwick Meets*. I based the programme on the idea of *Desert Island Discs* although the length of my programme was two hours. I had the privilege of meeting many famous and very interesting people. Well-known names included James Galway, Googie Withers, Richard Baker, Desmond Wilcox, Esther Rantzen, Valerie Singleton, Sue MacGregor, Rolf Harris, David Jacobs, Sir Geoffrey Jackson, Rosemary Anne Sisson, Bishop Trevor Huddleston and many more.

On one occasion, the crew of a Christian ship called "The Dolos" came to talk about the work of "Operation Mobilisation" which was a project to provide Christian literature to non-English-speaking countries. Eighteen months later, my very first guest, Jack Crawshaw who was then the producer of *This Is Your Life* was to show me what it felt like to be the subject of his programme, although I had no idea that it was going to happen.

I carried on working for the Disabled Fellowship Club. My latest plan was to raise money for a holiday for the Club members. This was eventually accomplished by the committee and, with the help of Ilford Rotary, a holiday to Bideford in North Devon was planned. Three ambulances and two cars travelled in convoy taking twenty-seven people, including medical support, to Devon. The organisational skills required were amazing! Finding suitable accommodation was no easy task, and still more difficult was mapping out the route with the most suitable toilet facilities and allowing enough periods for rest on the way. We stayed in a holiday camp. Bideford Rotary acted as hosts, driving the vehicles and showing us the sights of North Devon.

It was a marvellous holiday, and the friendships formed between Bideford and Ilford Rotaries and myself have remained to this day. The committee had achieved a great deal, and my parents supported me in every possible way. This was not always easy for Dad as he had divided loyalties, being also Secretary to the East London Spastics Society, yet I know he was proud of my efforts.

Through the work of the Disabled Fellowship Club, our people were really beginning to have a decent social life. We were so very blessed. It had been my firm belief that if the public could see what we were trying to do, they would give generously. Money has always come when we were really up against it. For that, and for so much else, I thank God.

Chapter Nine

"This Is Your Life"

It was the start of another academic year. I had been permitted to go forward to the next stage of my psycho-therapeutic counselling training. This necessitated being released from the bank one morning per week, which the management happily agreed to. This time the lectures were held above a church in King's Road, Chelsea, and we were now getting down to some serious study of the different schools of psychology — Adler, Fromm, Freud, Jung — together with approaches such as transactional analysis and the techniques of family therapy. I loved every minute of it. I particularly enjoyed role play and psychodrama.

One afternoon as I was returning to the bank from the

lectures, my manager, Mr David Wood, came into the switchboard room and said in his usual cheery way, "What are you doing on Wednesday afternoon, Berwick? I never know whether you are in or out these days!" I told him that I would be in the bank. "Good," he said, "because you are coming on a gin-sling with me." I told him to stop messing about and tell me what was going on. "Well you see, Lin, it's like this. You know the bank's policy of 'tell the staff as little as possible'? Well, that's it!"

I retorted by asking him to come clean, stop walking round in circles and rattling the bunch of keys in his pocket, and to stand still so that I could locate where his voice was coming from. "What it actually is, is that we want you to take part in a public relations exercise between the bank in London and our head office in Sydney, Australia. We're going to hold a Christmas party and we want you to be filmed making a call on the switchboard to wish everybody down-under a happy Christmas." I told him I had heard it all now and I wondered what else they could waste their money on, but of course I agreed to participate.

On the morning of Wednesday December 14, 1977, which was the day on which the filming was to take place, my mother woke me at 5.15 in the morning so that she could wash my hair. I told her I thought this was ridiculous. She said that if I was going to be filmed wearing headphones without my hair being set it would stick up and look awful. I had a splitting headache and hardly felt I could be bothered, so she said "All right, get back into bed and I'll tell Mr Wood you can't help him". I felt I could not let that happen, so I agreed to have my hair washed. Mother had told me she had taken that day off to do some Christmas shopping as she did every year. The night before she had, as far as I knew, been to the annual Christmas dinner and dance at the bank where my father worked. So, spruced up and ready for filming, I arrived at the bank at 7.45am, only to have the awful experience of one of my tripods snapping in two. It had snapped because of metal fatigue. I telephoned my mother in a panic and a spare pair was brought to the bank. Later that morning I was told a huge white van had pulled up in the road outside the window of the switchboard room and on its side were printed the words "Australian World News". Later that day, food and drinks and Christmas decorations were delivered to the bank and at three o'clock, when the bank doors closed for business, the whole banking area was transformed into a party scene. At 3.30 I made my way up onto the second floor for my usual toilet stop and was surprised to find the bank's senior secretary accompanying me, chatting as we went. At four o'clock a group of people gathered in the brightly decorated banking hall and a chair was brought into the midst of the group where I was placed so that I would feel comfortable. I was offered a sherry, but declined as I was not allowed to take alcohol with my medication. Then David Wood said "Well, just hold it so that you look as though you are enjoying yourself for the publicity film".

The party was getting under way when suddenly the bank doors opened and a squeal of recognition made me realise that something exciting was going on. Suddenly, I heard a very familiar voice. It was Eamonn Andrews saying "Hello, Assistant Manager David Wood". Although he is English, David gave him the typical Australian greeting of "G'day". I found myself thinking, "Oh, no" and saying to myself "Don't be ridiculous, he's probably come to surprise one of the Australian cricketers who bank with us" — yet a moment later he was at my side, saying "It's my pleasure, because I can say to a very remarkable young lady, Lin Berwick, tonight 'This is your life'." There was much cheering and laughter, but my knees had gone to jelly. Then I heard Eamonn saying, "All your friends here are invited back to the studio". So this was what the public relations exercise had been about! That 'dinner dance' which my parents had gone to the previous evening, and the shopping trip that my mother had done, were in fact rehearsals at Thames Television studios for this surprise. Although they did not know it, the people at the party in the banking hall had been selected by my mother because they had helped me in some way or had been a friend during my time at the bank. I said to my father "You rotten . . ., now I know why you bought a new suit!". This was not shown on TV but certainly caused much laughter. What a wonderful and totally unexpected Christmas present! I was so overcome by it all that I literally couldn't stand up. My father picked me up in his arms (I was much slimmer then!) and carried me to the waiting seven-seater Daimler limousine which was waiting outside. A huge crowd had gathered around the building as they recognised Eamonn, because they expected to see someone famous appear. Instead they got just an ordinary working-class girl from the East End of London who couldn't even stand up on her own two feet!

Eamonn was very kind and attentive. He kept asking me how I was feeling as we drove to the studios in Euston Road. He was concerned because he thought I looked unwell and when I told him that I felt sick, he opened the windows to give me some air.

On arrival, I was taken to the VIP room where I was locked in. This was done so that none of the people who were to participate in the programme would be able to call into the dressing room and spoil the element of total surprise. I asked to see my mother but was told that would not be possible. By now I was feeling bewildered and totally disorientated by the emotion and by the surroundings which were unfamiliar. I said if I couldn't see her, I would refuse to go on. She was brought to me without any further delay. She was laughing and crying all at the same time. Though it added to the excitement, the need to keep it an absolute secret had been quite a strain. If I had discovered what was going on, even just minutes before it began, the programme would have been scrapped. My parents, in fact, had known about the plan for some six weeks, although Thames Television had been researching it for almost a year. It had all started one night when Dad received a call from a Thames Television researcher. He was asked whether I was at home and when he replied that I was, he was asked to go outside and speak from a public telephone. I was upstairs in my study and Dad had taken the call downstairs. My mother instinctively knew what they wanted and said to my father "If they want Lin for 'This Is Your Life', the answer is 'No'." She was apprehensive about our personal life being portrayed on television, particularly on a programme which she thought might sentimentalise it, something which she knew I would hate. Dad told her not to be so stupid, that it couldn't possibly be for that. Mum told me later that when he came back to the house he was as white as a sheet. "You were right, you know," he said. "You did say no?" Mum asked. "Of course not," he replied, "if the nation wants to pay Lin a tribute, who are we to say no?" So that was how it had all begun. And now she expressed a sense of relief that there was no longer any need for secrecy. But I was feeling terrified and overwhelmed by what was happening. My stomach was somersaulting and I had to ask Mum for a valium.

There was a great deal of activity before the show began. I had to undress and have a belt placed round my waist on which were mounted two batteries and a long length of cable which was threaded up through my clothing for the microphone which was put on the lapel of my jacket. Then I was seen by the make-up department and before I knew it two and a half hours had gone by since the time Eamonn had spoken those magic words. It was planned that I should go onto the set in my wheelchair, but I wanted to walk because I felt that this was something worth struggling for. So Eamonn came into the dressing room and practised guiding me up and down. We then walked to the back of the set where my mother was waiting in the wings to help me up the high step. By this time the film of the "pick-up" was being shown to viewers. Eamonn asked me how I felt and gave me a reassuring hug. He started the countdown. Ten, nine, eight . . . and suddenly he said "Three steps forward and then turn right". Although I had to walk slowly and carefully because of my new sticks, I got to the chair on the set without any problems. I was in front of the cameras and there was no going back.

What the viewer sees is what actually happens. There is no editing on this programme. It was for me a very moving experience, and I felt deeply privileged that I should be given this honour. Thames had gone to a great deal of trouble. They had driven a Belgian priest friend of mine one hundred miles through the Pakistani jungle so that he could talk to me on the telephone. They brought family and friends from many parts of England, and even flew a friend over from Australia whom I had never seen before. She was the sister of an Australian friend who worked at the bank and she had sent me tapes to tell me about Australia and the family there. Thames brought her six months old daughter Rebecca over too so that I could have the pleasure of meeting the child. They also brought over a very dear friend of mine who had gone back to her home in Canada. Andrew Cruickshank and the late Hattie Jacques were also on the programme. Hattie spoke on film. She had known me very well as a child because she had been President of the East London Spastics Society. My dear friend, Andrew Cruickshank, was the President of the Disabled Fellowship Club of East London and naturally wanted to support me on this special occasion.

After the programme, I was taken into a small ante-room where champagne was on hand for me and my immediate family so that we could enjoy the opportunity of a few private moments together before we were taken to a large reception that had over three hundred guests. The guest list also included family and friends who had not been on the programme and all the people who had been interviewed together with all the people from the bank whom my mother had selected. So that "boring public relations exercise for the bank" had turned out to be something quite spectacular!

After greeting our guests we were all invited back into a theatre to watch a film of the programme. It was really quite amazing because at the time I was completely numb and almost unaware of what was going on around me. It seemed really strange hearing it all over again. Before the programme had started, Eamonn had told me that it would be seen by very many people. Afterwards he confided that it would be seen by 30 million viewers! To me that was absolutely mind-blowing. When we had all recovered from the shock of seeing how we were going to appear to the television viewer the following week, we had a wonderful party. Everything possible was done to make this night a happy one, even to the extent of a beautiful bouquet of scented flowers for me.

Just after 11 o'clock I decided that I needed to go home. It had been an extremely exciting day, and one I shall never forget, but I was beginning to feel totally exhausted. Mr Wood had given my mother and me a holiday the following day to help us recover from the excitement. We really needed it! A few days later the letters from viewers started to pour in. They were from all over Great Britain and Ireland. Many had found the programme inspirational, particularly those who were struggling to cope with some kind of adversity. We can never quite know how what we do and say will affect someone else. With television the effect is immediate and the ripples from it go on for a long time.

When Eamonn hands you that famous red book at the end of the programme, it is just the leather binding with his script inside. The completed book was delivered to me by chauffeur-driven car some three months later. It contained photographs from the beginning to the end of the programme. Most of the photographs are in black and white although some are in colour. The text of mine is compiled in print and in Braille and there is a sound recording on disc. (Not many people had videos in those days.)

There was something very special about Eamonn Andrews. On the day of the programme he had had the ability to make me feel that I was the most important person in his life. He wrote a personal letter of thanks in the famous green ink, which was his trade-mark and we continued to keep in touch until his death. *This Is Your Life* is synonymous with Eamonn Andrews, and I feel that the programme should have died with him. No-one will ever be able to take his place, however well they might do the job.

That one single programme reached more people than I will ever know and for that reason I thank God for it.

Chapter Ten

Shattered Hopes

I have probably given the impression up to now that my life has been devoid of emotional entanglements. This is not the case. It may surprise some people that a disabled person, particularly with such disabilities as mine, could contemplate having a happy and fulfilling relationship. The fact is that I think, feel and respond just like anyone else. I am as normal as the next person! It is just that my eyes and legs do not work too well!

My first meaningful relationship was at Dorton House. Adults tend to regard any friendship formed at school as "love's young dream" or "a ship that will pass in the night", but my relationship with Kelvin was important to me because he gave me friendship and physical contact when I most needed them.

Touch is essential to a blind person because the communication of affection by eye contact or facial expression is not possible. Touch and the tone of voice are therefore crucial to the development of any relationship. To "smile with the voice", for example, is one important way of expressing care.

In the early days of our relationship, Kelvin was extremely supportive. He helped me with my studies, often reading Braille text to me in his lunch-hour and after prep, because I could not keep up with the rest of the class. I had only recently learned Braille. When he guided me around Dorton House, he would pull my wheelchair backwards so that if he hit anything he would take the brunt of the bang. He was also very patient. When walking beside me, he did not mind my slowness. He was very tender and gentle.

We shared a love of music. He was a good pianist and we spent many happy hours together listening to and making music. He was a very sensitive person deep down, but he was afraid of letting people know this aspect of himself. I thought the world of him.

Kelvin had however a rather vague approach to life. Although he was extremely talented — despite his blindness he had obtained a BSc at university — he took life as it came to the extent that he tended to let the world pass him by. He became increasingly apathetic; he had become so introverted that he tended not to see things from other people's point of view and could often cause a great deal of emotional pain because of this. Despite the fact that he hurt me with his attitude to our relationship — it was first on, then off — I am sure that there will always be a degree of affection between us.

One thing that used to make me very angry was that he cared little for his personal appearance. Because people often have a somewhat uneasy response to blindness or physical disability, I am convinced that an awareness of one's appearance is vital. A good dress sense and pleasant manner can often be the 'barrier-breaker' that can lead to building bridges of understanding.

My parents were both meticulous people, so they were rather uncomfortable and dismayed by Kelvin's appearance. He would say that "It isn't what a person wears that matters, but how he is inside". I now know that he was fundamentally right. It is, of course, the person that matters, not what they wear. At the same time, attention to personal appearance is also an expression of respect towards another person.

After our relationship had ended, our friendship remained strong. Although we frequently had periods where we spent months apart and were not in touch, we could pick up where we had left off to the extent that he could say to me "I need a cuddle" and, happily, I was able to give it. Long after the relationship had ended, my mother used to get very angry about the way he had treated me. She could not understand how we could meet and simply enjoy each other's company as close friends. We would stay in a hostel in London, with a friend of mine who acted as escort, and would cram in as many trips to theatres, concerts and places of interest as we could get through — or afford — in a weekend. My mother was sure that I was clutching at straws. This was not the case. Kelvin and I were quite clear about the situation. In fact, Kelvin had become fond of my escort. She was a very pleasant, easy-going lady, very career-minded — I think the term now is "upwardly mobile". She was very clothes conscious, and "image" was all-important to her. Kelvin took her relaxing manner and pleasant voice to his heart and read far more into it than was actually there. This put me in rather a difficult situation. I knew by the way Kelvin was responding to her that he wanted this acquaintance to develop further, yet I also knew from talking to Sue that it was not reciprocal. Relationships constitute a great problem for blind people. They cannot "read" the body language of another person, so sympathy can often be interpreted as sexual interest. Social interaction is also made more difficult by mobility problems. In a crowded room, for example, what tends to happen is that a disabled or blind person is "put out of the way". We are stuck, therefore, with the person who just happens to be beside us! The freedom to approach someone who appears interesting simply does not exist. We have to wait for others to come to us.

Physically disabled people have so few outlets for emotional or sexual expression. For the most part a disabled person has to associate with people of the same sex because of the level of physical caring that may be required. There seems to be an attitude which presupposes that disabled people are somehow without sexuality. In my younger days the subject was never broached. I imagine that the thinking behind such silences was that it was best not to create a desire for something that could not be attained. Indeed, the thought of disabled people marrying was often regarded with horror. After all, there might be a possiblity that a disabled person would produce disabled children who would also be a burden on state resources. This fear is of course for the most part totally unfounded and, for those who are at risk, genetic counselling can help.

One of the biggest problems that a disabled person has to carry is that of not having the freedom to make his or her own decisions in the area of relationships. In addition, a disabled person will normally have very little privacy because of constantly having to be escorted, so couples tend to be always under observation. Parents feel they need to protect their disabled child from making foolish mistakes and being hurt as a result. Yet it is through making mistakes that we grow.

In my case I did find it hard to let go of the dreams I had had over Kelvin. I did this by pouring myself whole-heartedly into my work. I had completed the second stage of my pastoral counselling course and had the opportunity of undertaking further study. This meant asking the bank for a year off. I can remember going to the personnel officer to make this request and his saying "It has nothing to do with banking". "No," I proffered, "but I would really like to study psychology". After some long discussions it was agreed that the bank would give me every assistance to study; my job would be kept open for one year so that I would have something to return to if all else failed. They also provided me with four hundred cassettes for recording the lectures and helped me find out about re-training grants. I secured a Training Opportunities Scheme grant from the Department of Employment. I also received assistance from the Department of Employment with travel costs to and from Westminster Pastoral Foundation.

My parents were very much against this venture. They felt that I was making a very foolhardy decision. After all, I had an extremely good and secure job, and here I was throwing caution to the wind for a whim without any certainty that I had a new career at the end of it. I had however made my decision believing that I was right, and knowing that I must simply go forward in faith, taking every opportunity that came my way. Little did I realise that it would be through my qualification as a counsellor that my life would completely change some seven years later.

I was all set for my academic year, breaking free from the switchboard, when tragedy struck yet again. February 1978 is one month I shall never forget. In the space of one day, I was told that my right eye had to be removed and that my dog, Nicky, would have to be put to sleep. These were two major tragedies indeed.

To have the eye *removed* was perhaps the hardest decision that I have ever had to make in my life. It was the eye that I had once been able to use. To lose it meant

78

abandoning all hope that I could ever see again. It was in fact like going blind all over again. My family and I would no longer be able to play the games of "let's pretend" and "Who knows what medical science might bring?". This was a once-and-for-all decision and there would be no going back. At the same time, saying to the doctor "I can't cope with the pain any more" and hearing his response "We were waiting for you to say that" filled me with a great sense of peace and stillness because that awful decision was no longer hanging over my head. There was now no turning back. I agreed to the operation. I would be able to get on with my life without the restriction of pain.

I prayed to God, asking him to give me strength and also to help my parents during this traumatic time. I believe that the emotional effects of this kind of radical surgery should be treated in a similar way to that of bereavement because it involves a tremendous sense of loss. In my case it was the loss of expectation of what might have been. I grieved for the loss of my sight, knowing that I would never again have the hope of appreciating wonderful scenery or photographs of loved ones. I would never read a book again. It was incredibly painful.

It takes something like two years to 'internalise' such feelings and to be able to face up to them — if one ever really does manage that. If I am honest, I can only say that I have come to terms with my situation but I have never fully accepted it. Moreover, I could never fully express these feelings. I felt I always had to be strong for the sake of others, particularly my mother, because I could never forget her words when my sight failed: "I shall be able to cope so long as you don't say to me it's unfair and you want to be able to see". So I gritted my teeth and plunged myself into my studies.

About a year earlier I had begun a relationship with John who appeared to be sensitive and caring. He was introduced to me by the minister at my church. He was able-bodied and was applying for ordination to the priesthood in the Church of England. While he waited to hear if he had been accepted for the ministry, he worked at the church. Later my father got him a job as a bank messenger in the City.

We had known each other some eighteen months when the possibility of becoming engaged was mentioned. I happily thought that this was for me and I was delighted at this development. Yet there was some disquiet within me because, in all the time we had been together, I had only once met one of his university friends and only on one occasion had I met his mother. It seemed to me that he was embarrassed by my disabilities, and our relationship appeared to be fine as long as it was kept secret from the rest of the world. He would frequently go off for weekends to meet his university pals and they would have fairly heavy drinking sessions, but the idea of taking me never occurred to him. This would make me sad and give me acute feelings of rejection and insecurity. After all, if someone loves another, they usually want to tell their friends and show off their new partner. With John, this was not to be.

I was particularly sensitive to this because, since that time in February when I had agreed to have my right eye removed, I had been undergoing a series of tests at Moorfields. This was basically to pacify my father who was totally opposed to the idea of my losing the eye that I had once been able to use. To help Dad come to terms with this, I agreed to have electrodes placed on my head to determine whether the eye was reacting to light and underwater infra-red photography. This was done by placing a miniature metal cradle above the eye and water being poured over the head into this structure so that the eye was underneath a pool of water. That feeling of water being gushed over my head terrified me! When the pictures were developed, the consultant said "No wonder you were in pain, young lady, your eye looks just like a cake mix. The only part that is still there is the front." No wonder I felt as though I was going mad with the pain in my head. The pain that severe eye conditions bring is unlike any other because you cannot reach the pain to soothe it. You cannot rub it or keep it warm. In the end, the pain in the eye becomes all-consuming and the only thing you can think about. Because I had to lean forward every time I ate, I had constantly to stop and blow my nose because of the pressure. It was like having a streaming cold three hundred and sixty-five days a year.

I had the operation on July 13, 1978. It left me feeling pretty numb, yet I knew I had to pick up the pieces of my shattered life and begin all over again.

Two weeks after the operation I went to see Alex Cates, husband of Dr Wendy Greengross, who had very kindly agreed to see me at his private practice in Harley Street. Alex was an orthopaedic surgeon and I went to see him because I had been having a great deal of pain in my leg. He examined me and expressed concern about my circulation. He suggested he called in a professor of orthopaedics. I saw the professor and he asked me to go into hospital three days later. I said that I could not cope with that as I had come out of hospital only two weeks previously. I felt I needed some time to recover, not least because I am the world's worst patient! He was not happy, but agreed to leave it for a few months.

It was decided that I would have a bi-lateral lumbar sympathectomy. If I had had any idea of what I would go through I would not have agreed to the surgery. They had told me, however, that if I did not have it done I might eventually have to have my legs amputated. Yet again, I had no choice. For the moment, though, I pushed the worry of this to one side and got on with the first term of my full-time course. It was fantastic. We studied subjects such as psychopathology, clinical psychiatry, ontology, philosophy, personal development, adolescence, counselling case work and marital and family therapy. I had to work doubly hard because I was unable to take notes during the lectures due to the clatter of the Braille writer. So I recorded all the lectures and then played them back in private study periods and in the evenings at home. It was extremely hard work, but I really felt that it was worth it.

There were some in the group who did not take the work as seriously as I did. Some would pick and choose the lectures they attended, but I felt that if I was going to do this kind of work I must put my whole self into it to make sure that I gave any prospective client the best possible help that was available. If a person unburdened themselves to me then it was up to me to give that person my full commitment. I was so eager to learn that I soaked up the information like a sponge.

The first term ended and I had good, positive feedback from my tutors. I seemed to be holding my own quite well although I disliked intensely the group therapy sessions. There seemed to be quite a personality clash between one member of the group and myself, which spilled over into other lectures. But I assumed that was all part of personal growth; for group members to have problems with each other is not uncommon. I enjoyed a relaxed and easy friendship with others in the group. The lectures I enjoyed most were psychopathology and ontology. The ontology tutor was a Quaker. Her love of literature was infectious and her faith self-evident. She was a gentle, contemplative lady, very spiritual and motherly, not just to me but to every member in her class. She opened up the field of literature in particular, and I found this extremely stimulating.

On December 5, I was admitted to St Stephen's Hospital, Fulham, for my bi-lateral lumbar sympathectomy. I was told that it was a relatively simple operation and that I would have just a small nick on each side above my hip. I suspected, however, that it was not going to be as simple as that. How true that proved to be!

John would come into the hospital in the evenings after work to see me. On the morning of the operation, he stayed with me while I had my pre-medication and waited to go down to the theatre. That operation was the most painful, frightening experience I think I have ever had in my life. Although the doctors never confirmed it, I am convinced that I died during the surgery. What was to have been a simple operation took three and a half hours to complete.

As they went into the abdomen to get to the sympathetic nerve chain they found it was necessary to cut away more and more dead tissue. (We have a joke in our family which is that if the surgeon had sneezed I would have been cut in two!) When I had had the hamstring transplant in 1962, the surgeon had apparently partially impaired the pulse and the blood had therefore not been flowing into my legs correctly. This had caused extensive tissue damage which had to be removed. The idea of cutting and rejoining the sympathetic nerve chain was to enable the blood to be pumped faster down into my legs. I am no doctor and my facts may not therefore be 100% accurate, but I understood that to complete this delicate surgical manoeuvre the intestine and the lower bowel had to be removed and then put back after reconnecting the nerve chain.

During the operation, or perhaps just as I was coming out of the anaesthetic, I had a sense of a tremendous bright white light at the end of a very dark tunnel. My body had lifted off the table and I was free of pain and physical restriction. I was fully-sighted and I was looking down on my family in the room below. My family and John were there, and I could see that my mother was crying. She was saying "She is dead". I had a tremendous sense of elation, but also knew that I could not leave them like that. I felt that I was slipping away fast, breaking free of this world, and a voice was saying "You are coming to me", yet I was aware of my family pulling me back with their emotions. Another voice said, "You will come here one day, but not yet. There is special work for you to do". All at once I had a sense of my body being pulled back down onto the table and experienced tremendous anger. I wanted to be free of my painful body. Then, suddenly, I was aware of the most amazing pain that I had ever experienced in my life. I was screaming about the pain in my back. Doctors, nurses and a whole team were on hand and I was aware of the oxygen mask over my face, tubes down my throat, drips and tubes in my back, and I started to be violently sick, choking on the tubes which had to be removed from my throat. I remember saying to the nurse "Don't you dare put those tubes down my throat again". She told me that they must go back, but they and I knew there was no way that they would succeed in that. I was given morphine but the pain in my back was sheer torture. I had gone into acute spasm and all the muscles had knotted up. I could not get any relief either from lying on my tummy or on my side because the scar went literally all the way round my waist and down into the groin. I was drip-fed for eight days. I was being so sick in the end that I could not keep the artificial eyes in because the violent jolting of my head would cause them to fall out. I looked a terrible sight.

I was so intensely drugged for the first two nights that John stayed with me as much as he could. I remained on the critical list for several days.

Three days after the operation, John went to my parents' home and told them he was going to break off our engagement. They said that they fully understood, but begged him not to do it until I had come out of hospital. But on the Sunday morning — that was five days after the operation — John came into my room unexpectedly and told me that he wanted to end our engagement. I was still in a terrible state, with tubes sticking out in all directions. When I asked him why, he said "I see from what has happened here that you will take up too much of my time. I want to be free to go out drinking with my friends, and you will obviously stop that". I told him that things only looked bad because I was so ill but that it would not always be like that. He said "I don't care, I want out". In the middle of this conversation, the doctor walked in and was so angry that he literally pushed John out of the room and told him not to return. Two nurses came in and, when they heard what had happened, one of them sat on my bed and cried because of the way that I had been treated. Visitors arrived, Mum, Dad and friends, and I was in a bit of a daze. All I could say was "I want my mum". I was frightened and did not want to be left. Eventually, the doctor removed all the visitors and sat on my bed and asked me whether I wanted to see John again. All I could say was "I don't know". He said, "When I see the way you have coped with this pain during the last week, the way in which you have held onto the bed and gritted your teeth rather than scream, I think it is John who has lost, not you; and if John is an example of what being a Christian is, I am glad I am not one".

I did not know how I felt about John because I was too ill to care. What I did know was that I felt totally rejected. I knew my body looked a mess. It certainly felt a mess and, during those first days after the operation, I must have looked awful without my eyes in, but I was powerless to do anything about it. John knew about my artificial eyes, though he had only seen me on one occasion with an artificial eye out, and he had soon departed.

If you love someone, that love should be able to transcend body image but I think too that you would have to be emotionally mature to accept that concept. I think John saw himself as a knight in shining armour and he also liked the degree of fame that I had achieved as a result of my work with the disabled and my appearance on *"This Is Your Life"*. He seemed to need to feel important, and wanted people to think that he was doing good works. What he did not realise was that, despite my disability, I was not and am not a weak, pathetic figure but someone who is mentally strong, though not physically so. John's attitude had totally destroyed my confidence about how I looked and how someone could feel about me. His having said that caring for me would take up too much of his drinking time had been devastating. A pint of bitter meant more to him than I did, and at a time when I had most needed his support. Surely I was worth more than that?

My parents were so angry at what had happened that after visiting me at the hospital they went straight to see our minister. He was so appalled that he went immediately

86

to see John, who was not at home. He even waited until late that night outside John's flat, but John did not show up.

Complications were beginning to arise. My tummy was getting bigger and bigger each day. I looked as though I were eighteen months pregnant! It was impossible to tell the difference between my tummy and my chest, and the pain had become agonising. First I was put on a catheter to drain off any fluid. That did not work, so the air was literally pumped out of my stomach. Lying on my side to enable them to carry out this procedure was sheer torture.

One day I had a visit from the Rev. Douglas Wollen. He was the Superintendent Minister of the Poplar Methodist Mission which was, literally, across the road from my home. He came and asked me how I was feeling, but he did not get much of a response. I was too ill and depressed to bother with visitors. My minister had shown him the text of my first book, later to be called *Undefeated*, and he asked whether he could take it to the Methodist publishing house. I said he could if he liked but at that time I had no interest in anything. One of the things that did worry me, however, was the fact that I felt I would not be able to worship in my usual church any more because I would come face to face with John. When I told Mr Wollen this, he asked me if I would like to come and worship at his church. It was that decision to attend the Poplar Methodist Mission that was to alter the course of my life so dramatically. If the tragedy with John had not occurred, I would not be a Methodist preacher today. I believe it was God showing me that everything works together for good and, that even when we are in the depths of despair, He can give us renewed hope.

As I was recovering, I became terrified at the prospect of having the stitches in my back removed, but fortunately that went well. The operation, traumatic though it had been, was highly successful and for the first time in years I was able to feel the ground under my feet and had sensation in my legs. Sitting up and learning to walk again, however, were agony because my back muscles were so weak.

I came home from hospital just a few days before Christmas but I was only able to sit up to eat Christmas dinner and then had to lie on my back again because the pain was so intense.

I managed to go back to Westminister Pastoral Foundation within four weeks of the operation, but at first I was only allowed to do half-days because sitting was such agony. I was propped up with pillows and was on powerful pain killers to enable me to cope. I came through this period on sheer will power. When I felt strong enough, I rang John and said now that I was able to fight back, I wanted some answers. He said that I had "frightened the living daylights out of him" and that if what he had seen at the hospital was what caring for a disabled person meant, he "did not want to know". I told him that I felt extremely disillusioned, and that his clerical collar would be meaningless unless his actions expressed God's love. I told him I thought that he was in love with the idea of being a minister, and being seen as someone important. (I think he rather liked the idea of all the welcomes and the cups of tea that he would receive as a vicar!) I told him that if he could not feel compassion for someone he was supposed to love when she was suffering, I did not have much hope for his parishioners, especially those who were critically ill.

It was ironic that, before the break-up of our relationship, the Church of England had contacted the Westminster Pastoral Foundation for a psychological assessment of me in order to ascertain my suitability as a minister's wife. It might have been more appropriate if they had looked more closely at him! I heard later, however, that John had had his training deferred for a year because of the way he had treated me. It was not the fact that he had broken off our engagement, but because of the timing of it. The selection committee had felt that his actions did not express pastoral care. I could not but agree with them.

I now had to pick up the pieces of my life yet again. I plunged myself into work — it was that which kept me going. I switched off and tried not to allow myself any feelings. The studying went fantastically well. I was producing good work and holding my own in the lectures. All my emotional energy went into the work because I felt it was all I had left. We had had assessments and assignments, and I had done really well. When a student completes this part of the course successfully, they are allowed to take on some of the clients who come to the Foundation seeking help. The training is so advanced that the student is well qualified at this stage to do the work. When I asked when I would be given my first client, I was told that the Training Committee had decided that they could not let me take any clients because they did not know how poeple would respond to me when outwardly my problems were worse than theirs. They were particularly concerned that I could not establish or maintain eye contact. Once again, all I had attained was regarded as unworthy. Three years of work had led to nothing. It was on one Friday afternoon that the Rev. Denis Duncan, the Associate Director and Training Supervisor at Westminster Pastoral Foundation, came to tell me that the Training Committee had decided that they would not permit me to go forward to a further two years' training. This training would have entitled me to become a member of the Institute of Pastoral Education and Counselling. The only reason they gave for this decision was their concern that my disability might be a problem for the client. They would not provide me with any written confirmation of their decision nor was there any right of appeal.

I was utterly shocked. I asked Mr Duncan whether it had anything to do with my work and he said no. He also told me that my own psychological assessment had been fine. I started to cry and I could not stop. I think I cried for the whole weekend. I went to the Director, the late Rev. Dr. Bill Kyle, and asked whether I could do an "intake counselling" role-play. He agreed. This is perhaps one of the hardest sessions of counselling training that anyone can do because you have so little knowledge of the client's problem and yet you need to be a good facilitator to enable them to want to come back. It was done on a video camera with the rest of the class watching. He said afterwards that it was one of the best he had seen in that class, but the Training Committee's decision must stand.

I found that decision the most devastating thing I have ever had to cope with. I had been rejected on the grounds of my physical disabilities and I could do nothing about it. I felt completely devalued. The Westminister Pastoral Foundation's model at that time was based on the concept of self-actualisation and unconditional positive regard, yet in my case they did not live up to it. I felt betrayed, and totally rejected. Emotionally I was now on my knees. I had reached the depths of despair. The words of our Lord on the cross had never felt more real — "My God, my God, why hast thou forsaken me?". What was God trying to tell me?

I was confused, and in total desolation. For the first time in my life I picked up a bottle of tablets and seriously contemplated suicide. My mother was out shopping, and I held the bottle of valium in my hand for quite a few moments. But something inside me said "Don't do it, Lin.

90

That is the easy way out and your life was never meant to be easy. You are worth more than a bottle of tablets. Keep on going." So I decided to pick myself up and try again.

I could not bring myself to go to the leaving ceremony at Westminster Pastoral Foundation. I didn't want to go there and hear glowing things said about me, because I felt that would be complete hypocrisy and I might have just told them what they could do with their certificate! So it was sent to me in the post.

I knew that I just had to keep on with this work. I prayed about it and still felt that it was right. I talked to my counselling supervisor, Gill Brearley. We both specialised in disability counselling, although I didn't want to give the impression that, because of my own disability, I could only counsel disabled people. I see clients as people first and their disability is secondary. I had decided that I would apply for training with the Guild of Psychotherapy. I went through two interviews, for which privilege I had to pay £10 each time. I was told that if they rejected my application it would not be on my inability to do the work, but rather because of my disability.

Yet again I was rejected. The interviewer advised me to give up counselling altogether.

Travelling home in the car, I thought over what had been said about giving up and decided that I would not do that. It seemed to me that it was they who could not cope with the problems of a person with a multiple disability and I decided that, despite it all, I was going to take my equal place in the world. I was determined not to give up. Gill and I talked and she asked me how I felt. I said I felt as if I was banging my head against a brick wall, that nobody cared and nobody believed in me. She said that she could understand that feeling but would it not be marvellous if, while I was banging my head against that wall, the bricks started to tumble off the top? That image became an inspiration to me and has stayed with me ever since.

In the intervening years, that wall has begun to disintegrate. People's attitudes are changing, but it has been an uphill struggle. I later discovered that some of the tutors at the Westminister Pastoral Foundation had totally disagreed with the decision which had been made. It would have meant so much to me to have known this at the time. I have felt very often that I have been misunderstood, but I suppose there could not have been anyone on earth who was more misunderstood than Christ himself. So why should I not learn from my experience of this? I believed that this was my dark valley, and that the only way forward was out into the light.

Chapter Eleven

New Beginnings

My work with the Disabled Fellowship Club of East London continued. Our work was bearing fruit. We now had two ambulances and I had in mind a big publicity drive for the International Year of Disabled People in 1981. Weekly outings were organised with the ambulances throughout the summer months. The trips were mostly to the sea and the countryside. Many disabled people spend a great deal of their life staring at the same four walls so the Committee felt that, when the weather permitted, it was a marvellous opportunity for trips to the coast or to the wide open spaces of the countryside. This gave the disabled person a welcome change and a new degree of freedom.

After a trip in my father's speedboat in 1969, on a very windy day with a choppy sea, I had developed a phobia about wind and water so when this sort of trip was planned, I was unable to participate. I would just completely freeze at the prospect. I was not anxious when outings involved visits to the theatre, a concert, a stately home or an exhibition so I was able to attend these. Certain members of the Club who did not know of my phobia thought it quite strange that for many weeks in the year I was not seen on any outings.

As a result of our publicity, the parent of a handicapped child joined the organisation and offered to drive one of the ambulances. He started to have grand ideas as to what he would do if he were Chairman. My absence from the outings gave him the opportunity to make himself popular with those people who did not understand what he was up to. Although I was working had to raise funds to keep the ambulances on the road, he played on the fact that I often did not join in the outings to give me "a bad press". He sowed a seed of doubt in their minds as to whether I was fit to be Chairman of the organisation. His idea was that at the annual general meeting I should be voted out and he should become Chairman.

I had no idea what had been going on until the point of the election of officers at the AGM. Without any warning, I was voted out. I was dumbstruck at the way this was done in view of the fact that I had worked so hard for the Club for the previous nine years. Then, to add insult to injury, I was asked to come back on to the Committee as Chief Fund-raiser. I was too hurt and too angry to be able to accept that, and walked out of the meeting feeling devastated and rejected by all those whom I had tried to help and had thought of as friends. It was not that I minded being out-voted. It was the fact that all this had been done secretively and I had been totally unprepared for what had taken place at the meeting. To rub salt in the wound, as I was leaving the hall one of the members who had voted me out came up and asked me if I would try and get him a telephone installed free of charge. I used to take on board quite a number of these social welfare problems and, in one case, was instrumental in getting a person rehoused because of their disability. I felt that I would never do charity work again. This organisation had been my baby. I had nurtured it and watched it grow and I thought that as a committee we had done a pretty good job. But at least I had the satisfaction of leaving the organisation knowing that I had given it nine years' service; it had two tail-gate ambulances, the members had had nine years of activities and a holiday, and there was £700 in its bank account. Overall I did not think that this was a bad track record — especially as we had started with a loan just of £50!

So I had had another shattering blow to my confidence. I just could not understand what God was trying to tell me. I had been deceived, misunderstood and criticised. But when I related what was happening back to the scriptures, I could see that all these things had happened to Christ. What I had experienced was utterly minor when it came to the ridicule that our Lord had received. Perhaps these things were a type of cross that I would have to bear all my life. I know in my heart that everything that I did was done for the right reasons and I had reaped no personal gain whatsoever other than a sense of pride in my achievement.

Six months later members were telephoning me, pleading with me to go back. By then, under the new Chairman, the Club had almost run itself into the ground, but I did not feel that I had the mental energy to start building everything up again. Unfortunately, just over one year later the Club was totally disbanded. Everything I had worked for was wrecked within the space of eighteen months. I have often wondered whether I made the right decision in refusing to go back, or whether I was simply letting pride get in the way. But perhaps it was necessary for me to have this kind of shattering experience so that I could learn from it, grow and hopefully mature.

For the moment at least, it was back to the bank. How disillusioned I felt! All my hopes seemed to have been dashed, but the one thing that remained was my training as a counsellor, and I still had a job that would earn me a decent salary. Since the operation on my back I was find-ing stairs more and more difficult so the orthopaedic specialist advised my family that I should move to ground-floor accommodation. The plan was to look for a bungalow.

There are not many bungalows in the East End of London so we had to move out to Essex. This was an enormous step for us to take. The bank helped with favourable mortgage terms. The great disadvantage of this move was that we would have much further to travel each morning and that would mean an even earlier start. On the day my parents viewed the property, I was away for the weekend on a counselling course, but on my return they drove me to see it. It was a very spacious bungalow with a well laid-out garden. An extension had to be built to make the kitchen larger and to create an additional room to take my Clos-O-Mat toilet. It was really strange how this move to new accommodation was the beginning of a major change of direction in my life.

On one of our visits to view the property, the owner

had arranged for me to meet a friend of hers who was also a Methodist. She thought that this friend could then introduce me to the local church. When Ruth Page and I met, I knew that we would be friends; later she told me that she knew she was meant to help me. It was not until over a year later that I was to find out just how much Ruth would help.

As I have said, I had the call to preach in 1981, but study and supervision were not going particularly well partly due to the fact that the person who had been allocated to assist me seemed very inhibited and overawed by the practical problems relating to my disability, particularly when we had to travel around the churches. What should have been a relatively simple problem became a huge obstacle, but this constant flustering is typical of people who are unaccustomed to dealing with disability. They are often so frightened by it that they actually freeze and are unable to do much to help. Ruth could see that I was in danger of giving up my call to preach for lack of sheer practical help such as reading text books, writing essays and generally coping with the handling of large Braille books during the services, so she offered to take on this role and give me every assistance she could. She made that her own personal commitment to God and I can honestly tell you that, in the seven years that it took me to complete my theological studies, she never faltered. Her dedication was simply superb and I can truly say that if it had not been for Ruth Page, I would not be a fully accredited Methodist Local Preacher today. She must have dedicated some eight hours a week, if not more, to reading the texts, typing the essays and generally being very supportive to me. We have, as you might expect, become very close friends. My victory in passing all the exams was also her victory and now, as she assists me during services, she is able to see my development as a preacher. She is my most honest critic, yet at the same time is generous with her praise. When things have gone badly in my estimation, she has always boosted me up and encouraged me to keep on going. I owe my continuing commitment to preach totally to Ruth Page and for that and her very great friendship I shall always be deeply grateful.

Through my work as a lecturer and as a freelance reporter for *Disability Now,* I had gained a great deal of experience and something of a reputation in the field of disability issues. It was around this time that I was approached by an organisation to run a training course funded by ILEA for volunteers wishing to set up a bereavement support service. This was a three-month course of one evening a week, at the end of which an assessment would be made of the students by myself and a committee of well-qualified people. I was responsible for running the course and later for establishing the bereavement support service with selected volunteers. We had many influential and skilled people talking on the course and, with the help of supervision and videoed role-play, we were able to set up an effective bereavement support unit. In the end, because of lack of funding, it was decided that instead of psycho-therapeutic counselling skills, the unit would largely provide a service of tea and sympathy. I did not want to participate in this because I felt there were many organisations and individuals who could provide that help. It was the counselling of the bereaved that was all-important to me. So having got the scheme up and running, I left it to other people to continue.

I had done a great deal of lecturing and writing since the publication of *Undefeated* in 1980. The book had been successful in creating understanding between the disabled and the able-bodied. I feel it was this that was instrumental in my being made a Paul Harris Fellow by the Rotary

Foundation. This is the highest honour that Rotary can bestow. It is particularly significant because, when a local Rotary Club nominates a recipient for the award, a donation of $1,000 is sent to Rotary Foundation in the United States to provide a scholarship for someone in an under-privileged country. To me an award which is not given in isolation but which has a real purpose to it is magnificent. I wear my Paul Harris lapel badge with honour and pride at Rotarian meetings. For a woman to have received this award in the early 1980s was quite unique because Rotary is very much a male-orientated organisation, although I understand that this is changing. I think that this award meant even more to me than *This Is Your Life* because it was given in love and friendship by my friends at Rotary District 113, and the Ilford Club in particular. The friendship and continuing support of those many friends throughout Rotary, both at local and national level has meant a great deal to me.

I had another shattering blow in 1983. I had had a number of trips to hospital for various investigations to try to find out why I was in so much discomfort. I was finding it increasingly difficult to sit for any length of time. After many examinations, largely of a gynaecological nature, it was discovered that I had a hormone imbalance which had probably been exacerbated by the drugs that I had taken all those years previously for my eyes. I was finally helped by Professor Howard Jacobs at the Middlesex Hospital. All the other doctors whom I had seen had related my problem to my disability and had said there was nothing they could do about it. Professor Jacobs, an endocrinologist, said, "I see you first and foremost as a woman, who just happens to have a disability". He quickly discovered what was wrong, and was able to put it right. Sadly though, the treatment came too late to save my job at the bank.

My mother was due to retire in August 1983, as she would have reached the age of sixty. The problem was how would the bank cope with me now that Mum was not going to be around? Until then the bank officials had not really grasped the fact that someone else would have to take on the role of looking after me — but who? The situation was made more difficult by comments written on my mother's yearly report such as "We are unable to give this officer promotion due to the fact that she assists her disabled daughter who also works in the bank". Naturally, when people knew this they became reluctant to get too involved in case it affected their own prospects of promotion. Due to the time I had had out recently for various medical problems, it was felt that I should be retired on medical grounds with a pension for life, at the same time as my mother.

I did not want to be pensioned off at the age of 33, but I had no choice. I decided to use this opportunity to develop my counselling work. I started to talk to various people. Before now I had not been free to make myself available for counselling during the day because of my work at the bank, but once I had got over the shock and the feeling that I was being devalued yet again, I began to see how this could be turned to my advantage, provided I had the right attitude to it.

It gradually became known that I was now able to take on work during the day and eventually the referrals started to come. Counselling is a strange profession in many ways. The counsellor has to wait until the client is willing to contact him or her so earnings are very unpredictable, but most counsellors stick with it because they love the work. At first, retirement was really good because it felt like a holiday. But then the depression set in. I wondered what I was going to do with the rest of my life, and realised that the feeling of self-pity was starting to rear its ugly head. I think it is often necessary to go through this process of grieving so that one can think things out, rest a while to recover from the shock of redundancy, before gaining the strength to start new challenges. I went through all those stages — hurt, anger, despair and hope.

My good friend Dr Wendy Greengross came to my rescue, and in a most interesting way. We had had several discussions about what I would do with my life and then one day she told me of an organisation that she hoped to set up which was later to be called "Carematch". It was a project that came out of the International Year of Disabled People. Its aim was to have a comprehensive computer database of all residential care establishments throughout Great Britain, then to match a patient's specific care needs to the most appropriate residential home. A comprehensive computerised system was supplied from the Department of Trade and Industry in return for home-based employment for disabled people and then a large injection of cash came from the Greater London Council for wages, research work and general funding. It sounded an innovative and imaginative idea. Wendy told me all about it and said that they had the computers but what they now needed was a counsellor who had a good telephone technique to talk to the prospective clients about their fears of going into residential care and to help the carer or the client to fill in the computerised information sheet so that an accurate matching could take place. "But of course!" she said, "I'm talking to the ideal person. Would you like the job?" "You bet I would!" So this was the answer to my prayer. My telephony training and the counselling would be used to show people that Carematch was an organisation which genuinely cared about its clients and their feelings. It was not going to be just some heartless computer database, but a system that also had a human element.

100

I worked for Carematch for some five years. In that time I made many hundreds of calls from my home. One of my tasks was to contact every nursing home throughout Great Britain to ask whether they took physically-disabled people and whether they would take people suffering from strokes, motor neurone disease or Huntington's chorea. It was quite a task! But perhaps the most privileged part of my work was dealing with disabled people themselves at a time in their life when they had to admit that their disabling condition had got the better of them or when their loved one, who was also their carer, had died and their circumstances had totally changed. It was my job to deal with the initial enquiry and be a facilitator to the client to help them have the courage to fill in the form. Many of them felt that they were burning their boats. Losing their independence and giving up all the things in their home that they held dear was a momentous step. In many cases it was difficult for them to realise that this would, in fact, enhance the quality of their lives because they would no longer have the pressure of trying to cope. I also had to follow up the enquiries some three to six months later to find out whether the client had been successful in finding a suitable residential placement. Because of the fact that so many of our applicants were chronically sick I frequently found that in the time that had elapsed between the initial enquiry and my follow-up call, the client had died and I was dealing with the bereavement of the family or carer.

The work could sometimes be very depressing because it was not uncommon for me to have to deal three or four deaths in one afternoon, and I could not help but be touched by these people's suffering. Whenever the telephone rang I would make what someone once called an "arrow prayer" to God. This is not the kind of prayer where one sits down to meditate on what needs to be said, but a telegraphic request for help which lasts only three or four seconds. Everything I did for Carematch was given over to God. Each time I reviewed a new case-paper I would say a prayer that God would give me the right words at the right time. On most occasions He certainly did. I am sure that there were also times when I made mistakes but I hope that people realised that I was doing my best and working in the name of Christ.

My private counselling work continued and, as I have said earlier, I counselled both the disabled and the able-bodied. One day Ralph came to see me. He had lost his wife, Joan, just six months earlier after thirty years of being happily married. She had died of throat cancer. He was very distressed and was unable to overcome his grief. He was very much a family man who adored his wife, children and grandchildren, and his life had totally revolved around them. He lived his life through other people and was, I think, one of the most unselfish men I had ever had the privilege to meet. He was always a very strict time-keeper and never abused the session time with me. Only on one occasion did he go over time, and that was at my insistence. That extra time was all of five minutes, but that is how he was — very considerate of others. Although we talked of extremely painful things, I felt very comfortable in his presence. Sad though the conversation often was, I never felt that it was hard work or heavy going. We shared many private and very personal thoughts and feelings in our nineteen sessions. I think he probably told me more than he had ever told another person. He never readily spoke of his own needs. The only needs he could think of were those of others. During the months that he came to see me I had to change his appointment time on several occasions because of lectures and other work that I was involved in. He asked me how I managed to get to these appointments and I told him I did so with difficulty. He said that if I ever needed transport to get me to and fro, he would be happy to help as he had so much time on his hands. I knew that if he made a statement such as this he meant it. He was not the sort of person who would make idle offers of help with no intention of keeping them.

Ralph had been coming for counselling for some weeks when he went on holiday with his daughter Tina, her husband Vernon and their daughter Emma. This was a time of stress for them because they would be going back to a part of Dorset where they had been together as a family with Joan. He was quite tense because of this and needed reassurance that he could cope. He rang the night before he left, just to have someone to talk to and thanked me for the extra time I had given him. On his return from holiday, he brought me a china dolphin because he thought I would like the feel of it, which of course I did. I must admit I was quite overcome by this gesture. None of my clients had ever expressed affection in this way and I began to wonder what was going on. A counsellor has to be cautious of what is known as 'transference' and 'counter-transference' and be aware of the dangers. 'Transference' comes when the client feels inappropriate emotion towards the counsellor. It can involve projections of love, for example, or hatred or indifference. "Counter-transference" is the reverse. I obviously had to be very careful, but my heart leaped inside me when he brought me that gift. I enjoyed being with him, sharing his pain as well as his joys, although at that time a sense of joy was all too rare in his life. Our sessions went on during which time Ralph also suffered the loss of his mother. Although she was 83, she died quite suddenly, so in the space of a year he had lost two people who had meant everything to him. After his mother's death he decided he needed a holiday and in the time that he was away I was swotting hard for my first local preacher's examination which was to be on the Old Testament.

Ralph went walking the White Peak way. He had asked me the dates of my examination before he left and, on the night before the exam, he rang to wish me luck. I could not believe what was happening. I was frightened for him and for me because I knew in my heart that this was developing into something more than a client-counsellor relationship. What was happening to me? What should I do? I pushed my feelings to one side and told myself that it was the "transference", but deep down I knew that it was not. I talked to a counselling colleague who told me just to stay with what was happening. I prayed most earnestly to God for guidance. Was this what was meant to happen? I was being ridiculous. I must put it out of my mind. Our counselling sessions ended without any further expressions of friendship between us.

Then I was asked if I would go and teach Braille to a person in a residential home, some fifteen miles from my home. I was not in a position to pay the prohibitive cost of a taxi, and neither was Brian, my pupil. My only option was to ring Ralph and see if his offer of help was still open. Several weeks had gone by since our sessions had ended. He said he would be delighted to help me out. When I had prayed about my feelings towards Ralph I had asked God to reveal very clearly the right way forward. I had so wanted to get in touch with Ralph but would not allow myself to do this because of the ethics of counselling. I had thought about him often and wondered how he was getting along, and was curious to know whether I had ever come into his mind. Now I felt that this situation with Brian was a clear statement from God as to what I should do. Ralph took me over to Brian every week for four months. At first, I was just a passenger in his car, but

when I heard I had passed my first Local Preachers'
examination he suggested we should go for a meal to
celebrate. I was very nervous because I did not know how
he would cope with my blindness and my disability in
such a public place. But he was absolutely marvellous
and we spent a very happy evening together. After this, he
began asking me if I would like to go for a drink or a meal
or to the theatre or a concert. I had not had much opportunity for socialising and I readily accepted such invitations.
I was not expecting that anything would come from these
meetings other than just the sheer enjoyment of each
other's company. Whatever happened between us, I would
always have the memories of happy times spent together
so I decided that I would just go along with things and to
my great joy they developed in a way I would never have
dreamed possible.

Chapter Twelve

"To have and to hold"

The first concert to which Ralph took me was a Romantic
Classics concert at the Barbican Centre. All the ladies in
the auditorium were given a single long-stemmed red rose.
This had never happened to me at a concert before. Ralph
jokingly asked "Is this a hint?" at which I felt a little
embarrassed. The music was wonderful — Rachmaninov's
second piano concerto, Tchaikovsky's Romeo and Juliet.
How could I fail to feel the occasion was significant? I
felt as though my heart would burst. The music seemed to
be drawing us closer together.

The following week we went to another concert at the

Royal Festival Hall. Just outside the concert hall Ralph gave me another red rose, saying that he now had something to live up to. This was to be typical of the way Ralph would be, a bit of a romantic and very sensitive and generous. In the weeks that followed he tried to get me out as much as he could. We did all kinds of things together. I had never been out so much in all my life. It was wonderful. I prayed that it would last, but also decided that fearing it might not do so would not prevent me from enjoying myself to the full.

As the weeks went on we became closer and one day Ralph asked me if I would like to meet his family. He took me to meet his daughter, Tina. She was very warm and welcoming and Emma, her daughter who was two-and-a-half, was delightful. Apart from a rather nervous initial enquiry as to how she might help me, Tina did not seem at all uncomfortable with my disability. I must admit, though, that I was terrified. Tina meant so much to Ralph. How would she feel about me? I really believed that if Tina did not accept me our relationship would end. Fortunately she was very friendly towards me.

Emma was lovely. She obviously adored her grandfather. She could not really understand the concept of blindness, so when Tina told her to show me things she held them out to me. Ralph was sitting next to me describing what it was that Emma was showing me, but if I did not respond quickly enough to her she would get exasperated and throw the object in my lap. We found this highly amusing and, in her childish innocence, Emma helped to ease my tension. I was struggling inwardly with feelings of insecurity because of what had happened with John. I was now with someone who actually wanted me to meet his family and friends. My unconfident self-image was being turned upside-down. I was almost too scared to believe in what was happening.

The next family visit was to Ralph's brother Fred and his wife Barbara. Again, I was very nervous but they could not have been more welcoming. They opened their home and their hearts to me and it was wonderful. Ralph and I carried on seeing each other on a very regular basis. He was really becoming someone very special to me.

One evening I decided to test out his feelings by tentatively putting my hand towards his to see how he would react. I was so very aware of his recent bereavement and the deep love he had had for Joan. But I also knew what was happening inside me. It is very difficult when you are blind to know how your gestures are being received. Fortunately my hand was received very warmly, albeit nervously. Ralph had begun to feel guilty about the fact that I was becoming important to him. He had loved Joan so much and now he was becoming close to me and that was frightening for him. Because of my counselling training I was able to understand those feelings and did what I could to reassure Ralph. We spent many hours talking about Joan. I would tease him and say that he was getting some free counselling. I never felt uncomfortable about these conversations. It was as though Joan had become a friend.

One day, Ralph asked me to his home so that he could cook a meal for me. I had a great deal of difficulty negotiating the high steps, but we managed and we spent a very happy evening together. I wanted to express my feelings with more than a grasp of the hand but was frightened that if I did so it would make him turn away and I was terrified to risk it. I actually asked him if he would mind if I gave him a hug to say 'thank you' for such a lovely meal, and I told him that he had become someone very special. The next week when I visited his bungalow, I found that he had altered the steps into it, putting in an additional concrete base so that I could walk up them more easily. Here was someone who did not mind my disability and was even prepared to alter the structure of his house! He really did care, even though he could not express it. I just could not believe it. A week later I met Ralph's son Paul, his wife Lea and their son Tony, at Ralph's home. It had been difficult to meet them sooner because they lived in a block of flats with no lift so access for me was impossible. Paul very much wanted to do the right thing so as I tried to get out of the car he took hold of my hands to greet me. Unfortunately, I don't have any balance and I need to support myself with both hands all the time, so when Paul took my hands I almost fell over! Poor Paul was extremely embarrassed! He summed up his feelings about my disability by saying "When you are sitting down you are as normal as anyone else". I regarded this as a great compliment and wanted to get to know him better.

I think Paul and his wife felt a little inhibited by my profession and the fact that I was a Methodist local preacher on trial. They had not had much experience of being with so-called "religious people" and I think they felt a little afraid that they might say something unacceptable. They quickly learned to treat me as any other person and to accept me simply as Lin.

Weekends were fully taken up socialising with Ralph. We had now become much more than just good friends. We had talked and talked about the whole issue of our relationship. Ralph did not know where it was going, but he kept saying that he was frightened of hurting me. I began to feel that he was making assumptions about the fact that he was the only one making the decisions in this relationship, so one day I said to him "Look, don't worry, it might not be you who leaves me, but me who leaves you". The next day he told me that my comment had really taken the wind out of his sails because he had never considered that it might be me who ended the relationship. What I said had given him a bit of a jolt, and this had made him realise how much he cared for me.

We were growing very close now and the closer we grew the more I became anxious about issues concerning my disability. We had told my parents that our relationship had become quite serious. My father, in his inimitable way, remarked "I knew something funny was going on because he has shaved off his moustache, and I know that you don't like moustaches". I suppose we never give parents enough credit for being perceptive! I talked to my mother about my fears of Ralph seeing me without my artificial eyes. Occasionally they had fallen out in public, and I was always terrified that this might happen and that it would put me in a panic and greatly embarrass Ralph, and I asked Mother to show Ralph what to do. Her response was "There's time enough for that if you get married". But I did not agree. After my experience with John, I had to be sure that Ralph would not run away when the going got tough. I believed that the only way forward was complete honesty. I had put all my cards on the table and given him the opportunity of deciding whether he picked them up. I could see that the only way this was going to be resolved was to go away for a weekend together. We went to my friends Jenny and Bruce down in Verwood, Dorset. I had explained to Jenny how our relationship was developing and that we wanted time together to see how we would cope and they very kindly agreed to help us. They are a very warm couple and quickly made Ralph feel at home. Within the space of one hour of meeting him they said "Here is the key to the house, come and go as you like, and you are welcome to come here as often as you want".

They left Ralph to cope with all my physical requirements that weekend but offered their help if it was necessary.

On the Saturday Ralph took me to Poole. We wandered around the potteries and he asked me if I wanted to visit Christchurch Priory. I said no and he was surprised by this. I said that I just wanted to go back to the bungalow because I was desperate to go to the toilet. He got me home as quickly as possible and after I had sorted myself out he said "Well, I was going to ask you this special question in a lovely peaceful place, but you had other ideas!" It was then that he asked me to marry him. I was overjoyed.

Jenny and Bruce were thrilled for us both and, because they meant so much to me, the whole occasion felt even more special because it had happened in their home. We went out the next day to celebrate with a beautiful champagne luncheon. Jenny and Bruce had taken us for a ride in their Range Rover. Bruce was trying to show me what it could do when it went off the road; unfortunately it got stuck in the mud in the New Forest and sank to its axles. Eighteen people turned out from the village in the pouring rain to free us from the mud. Ralph had donned some ridiculously tight protective clothing to assist me, and Jenny was having hysterics describing the scene to me. And, of course, in the middle of this, nature called yet again for me, once again I was desperate to get to a loo. Ralph was learning how important loo-stops were to become in his life! (This story was later gleefully related by Bruce who acted as best man at our wedding!) Some months later Tina's second child, Rachael, was born. Two days after her birth, Ralph and I went to see her in the visiting time reserved for grandparents. I felt this might be a very private moment for Tina and Ralph so I stayed outside, but was quickly summoned by Tina who put Rachael in my arms. It was a most marvellous feeling. It feeling. It seemed to tell me that I was very much part of this family, and it was wonderful.

Ralph and I started to make preparations for our wedding. I had wanted it to be a truly marvellous day and, bless his heart, Ralph did everything he could to make it so. As much as possible I wanted the occasion to be as normal as any other wedding, but obviously we made contingency plans in case it was difficult for me to cope with the stress and excitement. I had always had this fantasy of arriving at the church in a white Rolls Royce. Ralph's brother, Fred, did some chauffering from time to time so we hired the car from the firm where he worked. The problem was, would I be able to get in it? The only way to find out was to have a trial run. Normally when I travel in a car I use the front seat because I need plenty of leg room, but I was determined that if it were humanly possible I would be like any other bride and travel with my husband in the back. Wild horses would not have stopped me from getting into that car! The trial run was successful so that was one problem solved. Now we had to think about the preparations for the church and the reception. We went to our minister and he advised us to book the reception first. We had a great time for a few weeks, eating out with the specific intention of finding out the standard of the hotel or restaurant before we booked our reception. Eventually we decided on a 16th century moathouse in Essex. The setting was beautiful, large reception areas, panelled rooms and a beautiful garden that guests could use if the weather permitted. Numbers had to be limited. We could have only fifty guests. I have a big family and many friends, so unfortunately we could not invite everyone. We decided to invite only our immediate families and closest friends. Ralph took me to a work colleague whose wife made wedding cakes and I chose the shape and patterning that I would like. We also visited a friend who was a florist who designed my bouquet which was to be roses, carnations, sweet peas and stephanotis. The scent would be divine! I could not wait for July 4 1987. Independence Day! This really appealed to my sense of humour because here I was breaking new ground and it was wonderful. Although Ralph was sixteen years older than me, it had never been a problem between us. The age gap made no difference to us and, moreover, I honestly believe that a less mature man would not have accepted the limitations of my disability. Yet again, God had answered my prayers.

I do not know how many years we will have together, but each one of those will be precious.

The church and wedding reception were booked and we now had to look for a property. Although Ralph had a home of his own we felt that it was important to begin our life together on neutral ground. We looked at dozens of bungalows and had many false starts. Eventually we found a most suitable bungalow that could be adapted to meet my needs, so it was all systems go.

Just three months before the wedding, tragedy struck. Ralph's brother suddenly died of a heart attack. Ralph was away on a course and I had to telephone him to break the news. He came home from Derbyshire at great speed, and we went over to be with Barbara. Even in this dark hour I had a deep sense of belonging. Barbara asked if I would take Fred's funeral service, and I agreed because he meant so much to me. He had been so loving and welcoming, even to the extent of cutting roses for me from his garden. He had never done this for anyone before because he believed that flowers should be kept in the garden. So I had been very privileged. Our wedding day would be tinged with sadness because Fred would not be with us.

Ralph moved into our new home on May 21 1987. He wanted us to spend the first day in our new home together so, although there was the danger of me falling over something amidst the chaos of packing cases and furniture arriving, I was there; I was so overwhelmed by it all that if I had fallen flat on my face it would not have mattered. It is a day I shall never forget as long as I live. Preparations were being made for my wedding dress and going-away outfit. I am not the sort of person who dresses up in fairy-tale clothing, yet equally I did not want to be practical that day. My mother chose the fabrics for my dress and the outfit. The dress was cream satin with a design of lily-of-the valley woven into the fabric. The shoes were going to be a great problem as I have to wear fairly masculine shoes because of my difficulty in walking, and I had decided that if it were possible I would like to walk back down the aisle after my wedding, provided my knees did not give way with the emotion.

On the morning of the wedding the weather was simply glorious. Mother woke me up at six and started to prepare me for the great day. She asked me if I had any regrets, and I said that I could not wait. My best friend, Jean, would act as my attendant and the service would be conducted at Harold Wood Methodist Church by my own minister, the Rev. E. Ronald Kemp, Superintendent Minister of the Romford Circuit. Friends from the church choir gave their services to us as a wedding present, other friends decorated the church with the most stunning flower arrangement, a friend from Thames Television made a video of the day as a gift, and June and Ron Taylor made a gift of the marvellous wedding cake. All in all, the service was fabulous and I do not think I have ever felt so moved and so proud as when I made those wedding vows to Ralph before God. As we went into the vestry to sign the register, Dad handed me over to Ralph and said, "She is all yours now". After signing the Register and the usual photographs, Ralph took my arm and walked me slowly down the aisle to the delight of our families and friends.

Our wedding reception went without a hitch and it had a beautiful atmosphere. The hotel had given us one of the bedrooms so that we could change. Ralph's children had found out the number of the room and were hammering on the door, shouting at us in fun. We let them in and Tina helped me change. It was wonderful that they could be happy for us and share in our joy that day. Although Ralph had carefully hidden the car they found it and decked it with cans and goodwill messages, mostly written in lipstick that we could not remove. Consequently we had shouts of good luck and a honking of horns most of the way up the motorway. We reached our overnight destination in Stafford only to find that we had been allocated single beds! I wasn't having that, and the room was changed. Two days later we went to York and had a blissful honeymoon visiting the area and the magnificent Yorkshire countryside. We returned to our home relaxed and happy, though I was very aware that for me a big test was yet to come.

Chapter Thirteen

Looking to the Future

After our honeymoon it was indeed down to earth with a bump. Ralph had taken another week off work to get me prepared for coping on my own during the day. I was absolutely terrified. I had never spent a whole day alone. My mother had always been with me, apart from the times when she had dashed to the shops and back. There had been no real need for such anxiety, but she regarded being there as her duty in case she was needed. Wonderful though that was, it did not prepare me for the trauma of coping on my own. So Ralph and I did what we could to alleviate some of my anxieties. We obtained a "Link Alarm" which gave me cover for twenty-four hours a day in case of emergency. The alarm is in the form of a pendant which I wear round my neck. The pendant is a transmitter which, when pressed, activates a receiver in the house which automatically dials an emergency number at a control base.

The controller will try to contact me by telephone to offer assistance. If they get no reply from me, they will telephone my husband or other nominees or summon help.

This service is a life-line because it gives me a sense of total security. Had the Link Alarm been unavailable, Ralph would not have been able to go to work because had I fallen, for example, I would not have been able to get up again. When I was visited by one of the volunteers who operate the service, I was told that I could use the alarm even if I felt concerned by noises outside the house. This is always a great problem when you cannot see. It is all right if you can locate the sounds and identify them, but when you cannot see, fear and tension can become magnified, so I am very grateful for this relatively simple yet very effective system.

Home helps became invaluable. Some were supplied by the council at a fee, and others were engaged privately by us. In this way we ensured that I would have at least one person visiting me during the day. Friends and family (my mother visits once a week) fill in the gaps.

I wanted my new home to be a place of welcome, where people would feel that there was peace, stillness and happiness when they entered it. I very much hope that I have managed to create that sense of warmth. It may not always have been convenient for someone to call, but unless I have been occupied in meetings or activities outside the home, I have never refused a visitor. I work on the premise that if I decline their request to call, I may end up with no visitors on the days when they are most needed. So all are welcome: it is open house.

It takes me approximately an hour and a half in the mornings to get up, wash, dress and have my breakfast; this meant that I would need to get up at 5.30 each morning so that Ralph could leave for work at seven. On that first morning, I was absolutely panic stricken. I just felt like bursting into tears with the fear and tension of it all. That period between 7am and 9.30 is, I think, the loneliest part of the day, for no one calls and the telephone doesn't ring. It was through this experience that I became able to empathise with those people who never receive a visitor, not even for a couple of hours, from one week to the next. What is more, I had never had to cope with any domestic task like making drinks for myself, preparing a meal, etc. The thought of it was truly daunting. The microwave oven is ideal for heating a cup of water. The oven surface does not get hot and there is no need for any pouring of boiling water. It is very safe for blind people but, even so, I had stupid disasters, such as putting the microwave on to "cook" instead of "heat" to make drinking chocolate. So many things ended up on the floor, not least of all my cordless telephones. I had one for my business line and one for our private line. I carried these in my apron pocket, but I soon discovered that normal apron pockets were too shallow and not strong enough to cope with the weight of the receivers. Consequently, every time I bent forward to pick something up off the floor, the receivers would fall out of the pocket and I would have to go through the very frustrating process of feeling for where they were and trying to retrieve them. I must confess the air was frequently blue, and I often had a heated argument with God! Why was He doing this to me? Why was He causing me so much frustration, such complete and utter physical exhaustion? I was so terrified of the whole experience of being alone that I was literally coping with life ten minutes at a time and praying for that doorbell or telephone to ring.

My mother's complete devotion had done me no service at all in terms of teaching me how to cope alone. In fact, in many ways, it had done me a great deal of harm because I had to come to terms with a life without her at an age when I should have been more independent. Difficult though it now was, marriage gave me the opportunity of developing many new skills which I would not have been allowed to do otherwise. What would I have done if she had died? I would probably have ended up in residential care. I would have found this painfully limiting because I would not have been able to pursue my chosen career and earn a salary.

Time and time again I questioned whether marriage was worth it? Would I not have been better to have stayed in my parents' tender loving care? I often felt extremely exhausted, but in my heart I knew that it was well worth the effort. I needed to strike out for my own independence and have an identity that was mine, and not live through my parents. I wanted to be my own woman, make my own decisions and make a home for my husband. In all the time that we have been married, Ralph has never become angry when I have dropped things onto the floor, or made a mess in the kitchen, or had something boil over. His attitude has been "You will get better with practice" and I most certainly have. I have now reached the stage where I am able to get the household chores organised, combining domestic tasks with work.

My work with Carematch continued and my preaching examinations were reaching the final stage. I still had the Christian Doctrine examination to come. It was the hardest one to do, so I put to good use that time in the early morning when Ralph had gone to work.

On the day of the exam Ralph took a day's holiday so that he could be with me and keep me calm. It was quite funny really, because Ralph became tense enough for both of us!

I had already passed three exams and all of them in grades no lower then 'C'. This grade is acceptable for application to the Methodist ministry so, despite the fact that because of my disability I would probably never be considered as a suitable candidate, I felt quite pleased by my success.

At my first exam I was allocated a scribe, but I think he suffered from writer's cramp at the end, so they decided that in future I would take my exams orally. Because of this I had the same examiner for three out of the four exams, which is very unusual. It was good for me that I was able to keep this continuity but he certainly made no concessions with his questions. I cannot actually recall them now, but I do know that when he gave me my ten questions the hair stood up on the back of my neck and I started to feel very agitated. It is often assumed that to take oral examinations is easier than written ones, but I found this system much harder. In an oral exam there is no way of referring back to what you said previously, and if you are in difficulties you cannot bluff your way through the paper. Just before the commencement of the doctrine exam, I decided to do a final "swot". Ralph was driving me mad because he was pacing up and down the lounge. He was totally unaware of this until I said "For God's sake, keep still!" "I don't know how you can be so calm," he retorted.

I wasn't! but what he had not taken into consideration was that I knew I had done my best. There was nothing more I could do and I had given it over to God in prayer. If it was God's will that I should succeed, then so be it. If not, then I would just have to resit the examination. The oral examination took two and a half hours to complete and I came out feeling an absolute wreck. I must say though, that the examiner could not have been more considerate. He even asked me if I wanted to rest between questions. I didn't, of course. My concern was to get on and have the whole thing finished.

I don't know what it is about disability, but people assume that if you are disabled you are also fragile. Nothing could be further from the truth in my case. I have an energy and a determination that I believe many people would envy. Because of my physical limitations, my mind has an explosive energy and no sooner is one thing completed than I have to strive for something else. Mr Goss, my examiner, very kindly put me out of my misery by telling me that he would recommend that I passed the exam, although I would have to wait several weeks for the official announcement. The exam over, Ralph drove me straight down to our friends in Dorset for a well-earned few days' rest. I had expended all my energies.

Two weeks later I was to receive yet another shattering blow. One Friday afternoon there was a ring at the doorbell and Dr Wendy Greengross called out to tell me she was there. I was amazed to hear her voice. She had not made an appointment to visit, so why was she out in Essex? Alarm bells began to ring in my mind. Something was definitely wrong.

I quickly discovered that my feeling was correct. Wendy had come to tell me that, as of June 30 1988, I would be made redundant. At the time I took the news quite stoically, but inside I was numb. Luckily Wendy waited for Ralph to come home from work to share the news with him too. When she left, I felt totally broken up, and wondered what on earth I was going to do now. I had worked so hard for *Carematch,* giving it everything I could, but I had been rejected yet again. Despite the very valid reasons that I knew Wendy had, I felt that all my efforts had counted for nothing. Ralph decided to book a concert for the next evening to take me out of myself, but I had little interest in what was going on around me. I felt as though I had a brick in my stomach. I couldn't swallow and I had no interest in eating. I think what made me feel so hurt was that they said they had made me redundant because of lack of funding, yet had made up the salary grade of the project manager and given additional hours to the part-time worker. I could see the logic of this because it meant that the *Carematch* operation would be under one roof. Arranging for batches of work to be prepared and sent to me was, I suppose, inefficient and time-consuming, but I had helped them with publicity, broadcasting and other things that were beyond my general job description, and I felt deeply saddened not to be a member of the team.

All that weekend I worried and prayed. Then the idea occurred to me to use the redundancy money to take a risk and try to become self-employed. This was sheer madness. Who was I to think that I could earn enough, or be of value to the general public? But what had I got to lose other than a state benefit which I did not want to accept anyway?

I talked to Ralph and friends about the venture. Ralph, bless him, said he would help and support me all he could. We would be all right financially because he was still earning a good salary, so there was no urgency for me to earn a living. So why not take a chance?

After three days of feeling in the depths of despair, I brightened up at this new prospect. Firstly I would talk to the producer of the BBC 2 television programme for the disabled, *One in Four,* and ask him if he could use me on the programme. Being a bit "up front" can sometimes bring rewards, provided you are certain that you can do the job. I had to start by believing in myself, because if *I* didn't, no one else would. A song that has always been my yardstick is "Whenever I feel afraid". The words of the first verse are very powerful:

Whenever I feel afraid,
I hold my head erect
And whistle a happy tune
So no one will suspect
   I'm afraid.

The result of this deception
Is very strange to tell
For when I fool the people
I fear, I fool myself
   as well.

Those last words are all too true. It really does work. I often get through difficult moments by singing this tune to myself. I also get strength from my belief that God has totally influenced my life. All things work together for good.

The producer of *One in Four* came to see me and we spent three hours in discussion, at the end of which he said that, rather than using me as a presenter, he would like to use my counselling skills to run a telephone counselling line for the programme. This would be an experiment to see how many viewers would take up the offer. It would certainly be a stop-gap until something else came up. Ralph was thrilled by the way I had been able to open yet another door. I think it is all a question of seeing what personal gifts you have and where best they can be used, finding a gap in the market and discovering if you are the person to fill it.

The job with the BBC would be a welcome stepping-stone and would give me media exposure. The producer had suggested the counselling scheme but it had not been confirmed. I just had to wait to see if his idea came to fruition. *One in Four* has approximately one million viewers, so in the space of one programme I would reach more people than most others would see in a lifetime. I prayed most earnestly that I would be given this chance and, when the offer finally came through, I naturally jumped at it.

I was very fortunate that, some two months before my redundancy, I had been advised by Wendy Greengross to find a suitable computer that could be easily adapted, because she felt it would help with the accessing of information to the clients. I had had several demonstrations of various computers and pieces of equipment, and chose the "Libra" Computer, which has proved to be absolutely marvellous. It has an electronic Braille keyboard with Braille display which works in conjunction with a conventional screen and printer. The Braille characters are converted into printed form.

After choosing the computer I was told of my redundancy, so assumed that the new toy would be taken away; that would have been terrible, because I could see how this wonderful piece of equipment would open up the commercial world to me and put me on equal terms with my sighted peers. Thankfully the Disabled Advisory Service, which is part of the Manpower Services Commission, agreed to let the application stand, despite my redundancy, so I decided to use this opportunity to become totally self-employed and set myself up as a Disability Consultant. I had my counselling skills, my abilities as a Lecturer and work as a freelance contributor for *Disability Now*. Since 1986 I had run a Crisis Counselling Telephone Line for *Disability Now,* sponsored by the Spastic Society, so I had a small weekly income, that precious pension from the bank and now a redundancy payment from Carematch. I would use this to set up my study with new worktops, printed stationery, telephone line. I prayed for God to guide me and it was now in His hands.

I had experienced quite a lot of emotional upheaval whilst coming to this decision and, of course, I went through the usual stages of post-redundancy depression. In fact, for about three months I was not the easiest person to live with! But Ralph stuck with it and has been enthusiastic and supportive with all my ventures.

During this period I managed to keep up with my studies. I still had one hurdle to complete before I would become a fully accredited Methodist Local Preacher.

This was my testimony and oral examination before the Local Preachers' Meeting. I was more nervous about this than the examinations themselves. It seems ridiculous because I was amongst friends and they were not out to trap me, but nevertheless it felt as though I were on trial. To have to give an account of one's Christian development and some of the sermons of John Wesley was not easy. There were questions on the Methodist Deed of Union, which is a series of doctrinal standards. "They are standards against which all theology purporting to be Methodist has to be tested" (*Groundwork of Theology* by John Stacey, published by Epworth Press 1980).

I am glad and grateful to say that I successfully completed this ordeal and was made a fully accredited Methodist Local Preacher. Both Ralph and I were absolutely thrilled and I could not believe that seven years' work had reached its climax. Things would seem a little flat after that, but at least I had my Accreditation Service to look forward to. This took place on July 21 1988 and was a great occasion. Harold Wood Methodist Church was filled with people. Quite a lot of them were my clergy friends from other denominations in various parts of London. My godfather, the Rev. Douglas Wollen, now in his eighties and a little frail, also managed to attend and this meant a very great deal to me. The service was wonderfully rich in the tradition of good Methodist hymn singing. The charge to the preacher was delivered by the Rev. Brian Goss who had been my examiner. He had asked whether he could be present at my accreditation service and I felt privileged that he wanted to be a part of this great occasion. I am sure it is relatively rare that an examiner keeps his association with a candidate alive, and I am thrilled that he did so and trust that he will continue to keep in touch.

Ralph thought that I needed a new challenge and decided

that we would fly to Scotland for a holiday. People often ask me what point there is in going to places when you cannot see the views, but they obviously have not realised that the sounds, smells and general atmosphere of a place are also very important, and the accents of people from different regions are absolutely fascinating. A change of environment and the opportunity to explore new places and meet new people are just as important for a blind person as for anyone else, even though it may cause a degree of disorientation. Rest and a break from daily routines and pressures are just as valuable to us.

One of the reasons I wanted to fly was to have a sensation of speed and power, but unfortunately our take-off was so ordinary that I was not even aware we were airborne! It was quite disappointing. However British Airways was absolutely wonderful. They knew I was a first-time flyer and they were aware of my disabilities and gave me every support and assistance. This has now opened up new possibilities for the future.

The approach which I had made to the BBC producer took almost a year to come to fruition. It was decided that we would offer a counselling service to *One in Four* viewers as a pilot project. It was marginally successful. Because I was the only person answering the telephone, the number of calls that I could deal with was limited, but nevertheless I feel it was useful at least insofar as it showed the viewer that *One in Four* cared about their personal needs.

Almost one year on, I have appeared in *One in Four* several times and have even found myself in the role of interviewer, which for me has been exciting. This whole experience has enabled me to discover that this is the direction in which I would like my career to develop. I have always had a fascination for broadcasting and any aspect of the media. My ambition is now to become involved in a programme which has nothing to do with disability. I would like to become a member of a team because of my abilities and achievements rather than because of my disabilities, although I recognise that overcoming my disability and making my way in the world is an achievement in itself.

Adjusting to my new, independent way of life was at times incredibly difficult. There were moments when I felt that it was all too much and I would have given up but for Ralph's marvellous encouragement and support. During this period I also received invaluable support from some very dear friends. I have now progressed to the level of being able to prepare the evening meal, get it into the oven and wait for Ralph to come home to lift it out. The one thing he forbids me to do is handle any food that has hot fat. There are not many things that he will not let me try, and that is one of the many things that I love about him. We are very much a team and he is happy to go along with the things that I am involved in, just so long as I am happy.

Disability often brings days of quite severe discomfort and many practical problems. Despite this, Ralph and I have a very loving relationship. His tenderness and understanding and the fact that he values me as a woman mean so much to me. Our life together has brought me incredible joy and happiness.

When one's life is full and one needs support, it has to be remembered that the carer has needs too. I am sure there have been times when I have expected Ralph to be Superman — and most times he is! But there are just a few occasions when he will remonstrate "I can't do everything at once". It is really important for me to realise that Ralph needs his own private space. Most of the time I am conscious of that fact and it works well.

Becoming self-employed has meant that I have needed a great deal of co-operation from Ralph. Since I received my computer from Manpower Services, Ralph has helped me become proficient in using the machine and preparing texts for articles, etc. Another new undertaking has been evaluating domestic products by testing them out to see how useful they can be for disabled people. We do not always need special aids. Often just a little thought in the design can mean that an object could be used both by the disabled and the able-bodied. I am trying to gain consultancy experience by visiting factories and inspecting products. Recognition in this field is slowly coming.

All these activities have been undertaken alongside my role as a preacher. My love for Christ needs to find expression in the secular world as well as from the pulpit. I believe that if Christ were in the world in a physical sense today, he would be doing very practical things to help those in need. Everything that I attempt to do by way of creating a greater understanding of disability is done in the love of Christ. God has given me the gift of the ability to communicate. I feel that not to use it would be a sin. Ralph has also played a very important part in helping to make it possible for me to carry out my work as a preacher. The sheer physical task of getting me ready and prepared for services, giving me a quiet time before setting out and helping me keep calm in the vestry is very important. Before a service I always become very nervous. I almost freeze with tension at the awesome responsibility I have towards my congregation. Yet, when Ralph pushes me through the doors onto the platform and puts me beside Ruth, the Lord takes over. I become a channel for God's message and He gives me the right words to say. On several occasions Ralph has stood in for Ruth on the platform. This is not a job he finds easy, yet when it has been necessary he has done it and in this way has enabled me to carry out my duties as a preacher.

Since our marriage we have been richly blessed. Because of this I felt I wanted to do something to express my gratitude to God. I have been conscious in my life that I have been something of a burden to people and so wanted to do something that would be useful to other disabled people and their carers. I wanted in some way to repay the debt that I owe to so many people for the loving care I have received. I prayed about what it could be.

Ralph and I have travelled around the country and stayed in many different types of accommodation. The adapted hotel room or self-catering bungalow usually leaves much to be desired with regard to its suitability for a disabled person. Ralph and I have suffered a great deal of frustration because of people's unawareness of steps or width of doorways. The more I thought about these issues, the more I realised that this was an area where I could put my disability to effective use. It would become an asset if I was to use my personal experience to improve conditions for others. I told Ralph that, after my death, I would like some kind of Charitable Trust to be formed in my name. Its aim would be specifically targetted towards making self-catering holiday accommodation more suitable for the disabled and their carers and families. I talked with my solicitor; he advised me that a charitable trust could be set up but asked me why I did not do it in my lifetime? He suggested that I would be able to put my experience of work with charities to good use in such a project. The more I thought about this, the more the idea appealed to me. I knew that God still had special work for me to do. I talked with Ralph, fully expecting him to tell me my idea was impossible, instead of which he thought it was marvellous. He had always wanted to be involved in the caring profession. Setting up the Trust would give us both the fulfilment we wanted. I talked to a group of Christian friends who had particular skills to offer — an electrician, a builder, accountant, lawyer, kitchen-designer expert, social worker and others with general clerical skills — and every one of them was enthusiastic and agreed to help me with this project.

On the 25th August 1989, the "Lin Berwick Trust" was founded. Our first project is to purpose-build a self-catering bungalow that will sleep up to six people. It will be situated in a country area, yet not too far from the coast. We feel that we shall need to raise £130,000 to build and equip this bungalow. Impossible? No, not if we get the backing from the general public.

I want this bungalow to have the right kind of specialist equipment so that a disabled person and their carer can have a trouble-free holiday at a sensible price and really feel that their needs have been considered and met. If I succeed in this, then my life will have been worthwhile. I will be putting God's love into action. I may not have kept my physical vision, but God gave me an inner vision that is far richer.

There have been times when I thought God had forsaken me, but I now know that He was there, holding me up and giving me a sense of purpose. I do not know what the future will hold, but I hope and pray that not just one but several bungalows will be built and will give pleasure to disabled people and their families.

If you would like to help this vision come true, please write to

The Lin Berwick Trust
47 Stafford Avenue
Hornchurch
Essex RM11 2EU
England

Lin using her Libra CPM Braille Computer in conjunction with the Brother HR 20 printer. Lin types on a Braille keyboard, the computer converts into script and the printer prints out the letter in normal type. The computer can work the other way round, converting script into Braille and displaying it on a tactile screen. (A Braille printer would cost some further thousands of pounds!).

The Xerox Kurzweil Personal Reader scans the printed page and converts what it sees into synthesised speech.

This equipment was supplied through the Department of Employment. The British distributors of the Kurzweil are Sight and Sound Technology in Northampton, and the computer is from Libra R W Limited, in Sidcup, Kent.

THROUGH PETER'S EYES
by Hazel Morgan

The world and its people as seen through the eyes of
a boy with Down's Syndrome. Hazel Morgan pleads for changed
attitudes to people with a handicap.

"I hope this book will be widely read for both its insights
and its questions"
Bill Anderson in *The Methodist Recorder*

ISBN 85305 305 7

DEAR STEPHEN
by Anne Downey

A grieving mother's letter-diary of the year which followed
her teenage son's suicide.

ISBN 85305 281 6

LOSS — An invitation to grow
by Jean Grigor

A book on bereavement for the bereaved and those who minister
to the bereaved.

ISBN 85305 269 7

SHEILA — A Healing through dying
by Saxon Walker

A husband's tribute to his wife's courage and faith
as she approached her death.

ISBN 85305 290 5

Arthur James, One Cranbourne Road, London N10 2BT

A DAY AT A TIME
by
Denis Duncan

A thought and a prayer for
each day of a year

ARTHUR JAMES
One Cranbourne Road,
London N10 2BT

ARTHUR JAMES'
Devotional Classics

GOD CALLING
over 2,000,000 copies sold, world-wide

GOD AT EVENTIDE
over 1,000,000 copies sold, world-wide

A TREASURY OF DEVOTION
GOD CALLING and GOD AT EVENTIDE in a presentation edition

GOD CALLING is also published in "de luxe"
and Large Print editions

ARTHUR JAMES
One Cranbourne Road, London N10 2BT